AGING WITH WISDOM AND GRACE

*For Jalee*
*With love, always*
*Kathy*
*xoxo*

# Also by Wilkie Au

Published by Paulist Press

*By Way of the Heart: Toward a Holistic Christian Spirituality*

*Urgings of the Heart: A Spirituality of Integration*
(with Noreen Cannon)

*The Enduring Heart: Spirituality for the Long Haul*

*The Discerning Heart: Exploring the Christian Path*
(with Noreen Cannon Au)

*The Grateful Heart: Living the Christian Message*
(with Noreen Cannon Au)

*God's Unconditional Love: Healing Our Shame*
(with Noreen Cannon Au)

# AGING WITH WISDOM AND GRACE

*Wilkie Au* AND
*Noreen Cannon Au*

Paulist Press
New York / Mahwah, NJ

Cover image by Yuliya Koldovska / Shutterstock.com
Cover and book design by Lynn Else

Library of Congress Cataloging-in-Publication Data
Names: Au, Wilkie, 1944– author. | Au, Noreen Cannon, 1945– author.
Title: Aging with wisdom and grace / Wilkie Au and Noreen Cannon Au.
Description: New York : Paulist Press, [2019] | Includes bibliographical references.
Identifiers: LCCN 2019005006 (print) | LCCN 2019013666 (ebook) | ISBN 9781587688577 (ebook) | ISBN 9780809154623 (pbk. : alk. paper)
Subjects: LCSH: Aging—Religious aspects—Christianity. | Older people—Religious life.
Classification: LCC BV4580 (ebook) | LCC BV4580 .A895 2019 (print) | DDC 248.8/5—dc23
LC record available at https://lccn.loc.gov/2019005006

ISBN 978-0-8091-5462-3 (paperback)
ISBN 978-1-58768-857-7 (e-book)

Published by Paulist Press
997 Macarthur Boulevard
Mahwah, New Jersey 07430
www.paulistpress.com

Printed and bound in the
United States of America

# CONTENTS

# ACKNOWLEDGMENTS

We are indebted to Bernadette Miles, cofounder of Kardia Spiritual Formation Center in Melbourne, Australia, and member of the Coordinating Council of Spiritual Directors International, for writing the foreword.

# FOREWORD

You picked up this book! That suggests you may be entering a certain age or perhaps live and work with people who are navigating the aging process. Either way, you will soon discover that aging in the twenty-first century—an era of constant change—requires a new mindset, and the book you have in your hands will offer you just that.

The foundations of the world as we have known it are being shaken to the core. Changes in our spiritual, political, institutional, educational, familial, scientific, and financial systems, to name a few, are extensive and unpredictable. The generation entering the aging phase of life today have witnessed change like no other generation before them. You probably have parents who were awed by the speed of freeway travel and witnessed the first television come into their home. Now our grandchildren have instant communication to anywhere on the planet at all times and will soon be transported in driverless cars. Mobile phones have become an extension of the human brain, providing access to information in an instant. What might be next?

You may be feeling the desire to resist change or exhausted by the rate of change. The truth is that in the twenty-first century, we also live in a time of great opportunity with unprecedented resourcefulness and creativity. Can we tap into this creativity and resourcefulness to reimagine what it means to age with wisdom and grace?

Wilkie and Noreen do just that as they challenge us to ask, "What does *aging well* mean today?" They invite us to consider whether we view successful aging as the absence of disease and disability; or could we dare to ask if we are satisfied with the quality of our lives? Are we living to our full potential, regardless of our aging stage?

Wilkie and Noreen reject the notion of aging purely as a time of decline, recognizing that people can continue to develop and change in ways that are enriching and satisfying in every stage of life.

Drawing on their deep wisdom and personal experience, Wilkie and Noreen explore the many facets of aging, including loss, grief, regret, resentment, aches and pains, our expiration date, faith, and rummaging for God in times of challenge. They uncover how faith can play a significant role in our well-being during the aging process and help us to consider any fears we might be facing as we near the completion of our lives.

I first met Wilkie and Noreen in 2013 when they came to Australia to work with us in our Centers of Ignatian Spirituality. Their wisdom and grace permeate every aspect of their being, and this is reflected deeply in every page of their writing. In sharing their wisdom about the possibilities we create if we become conscious of the choices we make in the journey of aging, they give a tremendous gift to us all. In receiving the gifts of this book, may you discover the journey of aging as one of being filled with wisdom and grace.

*Bernadette Miles, PhD*
Cofounder of *Kardia* Spiritual Formation Centre, Australia
Member, Coordinating Council of Spiritual Directors International

# INTRODUCTION
## Graceful Aging

A human being would certainly not grow to be
seventy or eighty years old if this longevity had no
meaning for the species. The afternoon of human
life must also have a significance of its own and
cannot be merely a pitiful appendage to life's
morning.

—Carl Jung, *Modern Man in Search of a Soul*

All of us, if we are lucky, are going to find ourselves in "the afternoon
of life." Life-expectancy statistics tell us we can expect to live well
into our eighties or nineties, unless a fatal disease or accident befalls
us. Moreover, at least half of us born in the developed world today
can expect to live to be one hundred.[1] This increased longevity
challenges us to consider this stage of life more thoughtfully. Aging
cannot be defined too narrowly. It includes a very wide range of
ages. There are big differences between the oldest of the old—
people in their late eighties and nineties—and younger old people
in their late sixties and seventies. While we cannot keep the years
from piling up or prevent our eventual death, we can nevertheless
consider the question of what aging well means to us.

# AGING WITH WISDOM AND GRACE

What constitutes successful aging is a very subjective matter. It is not accurate to suggest that there is some norm or universal standard, for example, that all older people should be active, creative, socially involved, able-bodied, and spiritually evolved. Insisting on a universal norm would be as prejudicial as ageist stereotypes.[2] When reflecting on aging successfully, we must consider individual differences and circumstances, such as physical health and the availability of opportunity based on income, education, social status, and social support. Such factors influence how much control people have over how they age. In the past, a medical model viewed successful aging as the absence of disease and disability. A more recent—and more comprehensive—understanding suggests that successful aging has to do with an individual's felt satisfaction. It has to do with one's ability to adapt to physical and functional changes while maintaining a connection to other people and a sense of meaning and purpose. It's about whether a person is satisfied with one's quality of life.

How does our culture view getting older? Popular magazines and antiaging ads tell us that successful aging means not looking one's age. Many Americans view aging negatively as declining middle age. Getting old means being sidelined and losing our role in society. It means deteriorating health and loss of independence, identity, and worth. From this point of view, aging well then becomes doing whatever we can to slow down the inevitable slide toward decrepitude and misery that follows middle age. It's no wonder that so many people hate the idea of getting old and fight against it by ignoring it. If you've picked up this book, you probably aren't in denial about getting old and most likely are looking for ideas that can help you navigate this important and final stage of life with as much joy and meaning as possible.

Rather than a stage of decline, aging for most people, at least prior to age eighty, is "a relatively neutral balance of gains and losses that is experienced as a gentle slowing down that allows them to maintain their preferred lifestyle."[3] Burdensome as they may be, physical limitations and even chronic health problems may have little long-term effect on happiness. We tend to adjust to them.[4] It would be a mistake, then, to see aging as a period of inexorable decline in health and vitality. What more often occurs is a long period of relative equilibrium with very gradual changes in health that we can adapt to. This phase of aging is ripe with possibilities for personal development and growth.[5] The sheer number of people living into old age makes it important to understand more about the potential for this stage of life. If one retires at sixty-five or seventy and lives for another twenty or thirty years, this is a period as long as childhood and adolescence.

The reality is that we have some choice about how we approach aging. By not internalizing negative stereotypes of aging, we are free to discover the new possibilities that this stage ushers in. There is a striking correlation between our attitude toward growing older and how we fare in our later years, with effects starting as early as middle age, according to Yale psychiatrist Becca R. Levy. Levy and her colleagues found that "people with positive views of old age had lower blood pressure, less stress, better physical balance, and were more likely to develop healthy habits and get regular medical care. They also lived an average of seven and a half years longer—a genuine fountain of youth, available without a prescription."[6]

There is no doubt that the afternoon of life has its challenges and fears. But it is also a time of new opportunities for growth and satisfaction. As the poet Henry Wadsworth Longfellow aptly states, "Age is an opportunity no less than youth itself, though in another dress. And as the evening twilight fades away, the sky is filled with stars invisible by day." Similarly, Carl Jung insisted, "The afternoon of life is just as full of meaning as the morning; only its meaning and purpose are different."[7] It should not be viewed merely as "a pitiful appendage to life's morning" or just as the passing of time until death. Echoing Jung, Joan Chittister writes, "If we decide that life is over once the accoutrements of middle age are over—the career, the title, the children, the climb up the social ladder—that there is nothing else worth doing, that the very definition of who we are has been summarily foreclosed, then of course it will be. We have ended ourselves."[8] According to Jung, old age provides us with the opportunity to develop the richness of who we are as persons:

- to integrate valuable parts of ourselves that were neglected or underdeveloped earlier in life;
- to feel a greater wholeness by reviewing our life and reconciling ourselves with past regrets and failures, as well as savoring our joys and successes;
- to root our identity less on external norms of physical appearance and material possessions and more on internal qualities and values that reflect our spiritual nature;
- to free ourselves from bondage to external approval and egocentric achievements and to live more deeply out of our authentic self;
- to appreciate the wisdom we have gained through the years and to recognize how we can contribute to making life better for others;
- to energize our lives with a renewed sense of what gives life meaning.

By pointing out these possibilities for personal growth, Jungian psychology provides an important perspective that gives meaning and significance to growing old. Pause for just a moment and ask yourself what comes to mind when you think about such possibilities. For example, what interests or aspects of yourself did you put aside in the first half of your life that you might want to develop?

Influenced by Carl Jung, Swiss gerontologist Lars Tornstam has developed a theory of positive aging called *gero-transcendence*.[9] Based on his own extensive research, he suggests that aging is a natural developmental process toward maturity and wisdom that brings about a change in one's sense of self and outlook on life. Rejecting the notion of aging as a time of decline, he believes that people can continue to develop and change in ways that are enriching and satisfying. Many of Tornstam's findings challenge us to rethink our view of healthy aging. Some of the signs of healthy aging in the framework of gero-transcendence are the following:

- a decreased preoccupation with one's body;
- a decrease in self-centeredness and an increased desire to understand oneself;
- a greater desire for solitude and meditation;
- less interest in superficial relationships;
- less need for approval and prestige and a greater desire to be one's authentic self;
- a greater acceptance of ambiguity and tolerance for change;
- an increase in one's ability to accept others without judgment;
- a greater acceptance of life as mystery;
- a decreased fear of death;
- a greater appreciation for the ordinary joys of life;
- an increased concern for future generations;
- a greater sense of oneness with all creation.

Jung's and Tornstam's developmental context for late-life growth highlights what most adults by late middle age have already discovered: "that the modern prescription for life meaning—materialism and social achievement—do not meet the needs of the soul."[10] Old age and retirement give us the opportunity to reclaim values that have dropped through the cracks because of the demands of work and family life. To make full use of this opportunity to reclaim these values—such as intimacy and friendship, leisure and creativity—is to live vibrantly until the end. Living as fully as we can is the best preparation for a happy death. Palliative caregivers tell us that among the top regrets of the dying are such sentiments as the following: "I wish I had stayed in touch with my friends"; "I wish I'd had the courage to express my feelings"; "I wish I hadn't worked so hard."[11] Or, as is often repeated in twelve-step meetings, "No one when dying ever regrets not having spent more time at the office!"

# Challenges as We Age

A realistic look at aging must also acknowledge that "old age is no place for sissies"—as Bette Davis is famous for reminding us. In her typically irreverent and humorous way, she captures what we all experience as we age. Along with the blessings of increased longevity come heartaches and challenges. As we get older, we may experience hardships that are life-changing, for example:

- the death of a sibling or a spouse
- the early death of a child
- physical diminishment and disability
- the onset of chronic illness (cancer, diabetes, heart disease)
- loneliness and sadness due to separation from family and close friends
- loss of self-esteem and boredom in retirement

It is normal to feel stressed, sad, or overwhelmed by such losses. Stressful life events require us to figure out how to continue to live vibrantly without succumbing to discouragement and sadness.

Our hope in writing this book is to offer the resources of Christian spirituality that can help us to adapt to the changes inherent in growing older in ways that allow us "to choose life." "Today...I am offering you life or death, blessing or curse," Moses proclaimed. "Choose life, then, so that you and your descendants may live, in the love of Yahweh your God, obeying his voice, clinging to him, for in this your life consists" (Deut 30:19–20 NJB). To choose life when enjoying robust health and exciting prospects comes easily. The morning of life is flush with youthful dreams and hopes. If we work at it, those dreams and hopes can survive the onslaughts of "the noonday devil," those midlife disillusionments and disappointments that tempt us to give up on life. And in the afternoon and evening of life, we must find within ourselves the resources to say yes to life amid the many challenges that will face us.

The anonymous prayer of a seventeenth-century nun illustrates a stance toward aging that is at once wise and lighthearted:

> Lord, thou knowest better than I know myself that I am growing older and will someday be old. Keep me from the fatal habit of thinking I must say something on every subject and on every occasion. Release me from craving to straighten out everybody's affairs. Make me thoughtful but not moody; helpful but not bossy. With my vast store of wisdom, it seems a pity not to use it all, but Thou knowest Lord, that I want a few friends at the end.
>
> Keep my mind free from the recital of endless details; give me wings to get to the point. Seal my lips on my aches and pains. They are increasing and love of rehearsing them is becoming sweeter as the years go by. I dare not ask for grace enough to enjoy the tales of other's pains, but help me to endure them with patience. I dare not ask for improved memory, but for a growing humility and a lessening cocksureness when my memory seems to clash with the memories of others. Teach me the glorious lesson that occasionally I may be mistaken.
>
> Keep me reasonably sweet; I do not want to be a saint—some of them are so hard to live with—but a sour old person is one of the crowning works of the Devil. Give me the ability to see good things in unexpected

places and talents in unexpected people. And, give me,
O Lord, the grace to tell them so.
Amen.[12]

This delightful prayer reflects the thoughts of Pope Francis in his Pentecost homily of 2018, "The Spirit keeps our hearts young—a renewed youth. Youth, for all our attempts to prolong it, sooner or later fades away; the Spirit, instead, prevents the only kind of aging that is unhealthy: namely, growing old within."

# Chapter 1

# AGING AND FAITH

Life's challenges mock and then destroy a faith
that rests on correct thinking…and clear the
clutter so we can see more clearly that faith calls
for trust instead.

—Peter Enns, *The Sin of Certainty*

"Though many Americans proclaim a faith in God, their spiritual lives are restricted to church, or temple, or mosque, and rarely, if ever, applied to the question of aging."[1] This provocative observation by Ram Dass leads us to wonder about the role of faith in aging well. What, if anything, does faith have to offer when it comes to dealing with the issues and challenges that old age presents?

Psychiatrist George E. Valliant, who directed Harvard's famous longitudinal study of human development and aging,[2] found that faith "is clearly associated with aging well" because it brings about an increase of hope and love, emotions that have proven to decrease pain and alleviate suffering.[3] He distinguishes between faith as belief (religion) and faith as trust in God or a higher power (spirituality). Spirituality and religion differ in important ways: religion has to do with identification with a group's doctrine, values, and

1

tradition. Spirituality refers to an individual's personal experience and connection to something larger than the self (God or a higher power) with feelings of awe, gratitude, compassion, hope, forgiveness, and faith as trust.[4] Valliant discovered, to his surprise, that many became more spiritual and less concerned with religious dogma as they aged. While not discounting the value that religious participation can bring to an individual's life, he argues that it is spirituality that increases trust, hope, and love—emotions that enable one to thrive in the midst of the losses and challenges that old age brings. Following decades of research, Valliant came to the conclusion that it is spirituality that leads to successful aging, with or without the aid of religion. Religion can contribute to aging well when it provides a portal through which trust is fostered.

Rabbi Rami Shapiro, writing about faith's contribution to spiritual development, also distinguishes between religion and spirituality. Religion, he asserts, is about belonging, community, shared values, shared rituals and mutual support." Understood in this sense, religion greatly benefits elders, many of whom feel isolated and disconnected from life around them. Additionally, religion can serve as "a container in which spiritual practices are preserved and passed on." Such practices allow us to develop a spirituality, which in Shapiro's words, is about "living life without a net, forever surrendered to reality and meeting each moment with curiosity, wonder, gratitude, justice, humility, and love."[5]

In our view, religion, at its best, can help healthy aging by providing resources for spiritual living; at its worst, religion can hinder access to the Sacred through rigid dogmas and restrictions. A vibrant spirituality that enables us to make a personal connection to the Sacred and to experience God in all circumstances of life is an invaluable support to aging well. Faith loses its rich significance for our lives if we reduce it to simple fidelity to dogma, because having faith involves so much more than having "correct beliefs." Faith "does not mean faithfulness to *statements* about

God, whether biblical, doctrinal, or creedal. Rather it means faithfulness to the God to whom the Bible and creeds and doctrines point," biblical scholar Marcus Borg rightly asserts.[6] Doctrinal statements are our human attempts to understand the Mystery of God who always outstrips the capacity of our finite minds to fully comprehend.[7] While the Bible is full of valuable images that convey Jesus's understanding of God, we realize that these images are not meant to be taken literally, for in essence God's unlikeness to anything in the created universe is total. Yet, as analogies or metaphors, they communicate important truths about the Mystery of God. For example, the biblical understanding of God as our Father portrays how God loves and treasures each and every human being. God is Spirit, neither male nor female, yet Scripture illustrates the unconditional love of God with a paternal image. By calling God "Father," the gospel proclaims that "the ultimate ground of reality is love" and that God is forever "for us." To acknowledge God as Father is "to become aware of oneself not as stranger, not as an outsider or alienated person, but as [one] who belongs."[8] To insist, however, that faith requires conceiving of God as a man is to blur the underlying message of God as Love. Biblical and creedal statements are meant to point us to God, not be the center of attention themselves. As an ancient Chinese proverb warns, "Only the fool stares at the finger when it is pointing to the moon."

Sometimes people feel distant from God because they question beliefs they were taught as children or disagree with certain Church teachings—like papal infallibility, the ban on artificial contraception, and the exclusion of women from priestly ordination. Their critical stance puts them at odds with the institutional church and makes them feel that they have lost their faith. "The deeper problem here," observes biblical theologian Peter Enns, "is the unspoken need for our thinking about God [and doctrine] to be right *in order* to have a joyful, freeing, healing, and meaningful faith."[9]

# Faith Is More than Believing

Theologically, faith involves much more than orthodox thinking or institutional conformity, though people who are solely focused on orthodoxy seem to think about faith exclusively in this way. Faith as believing the right things is only one way of understanding faith. In addition to faith as beliefs, faith as trust and faith as a way of perceiving God and the whole of reality are two other important ways to understand faith.[10] Considering faith in these two ways can increase our appreciation of how faith can be a reliable source of support and comfort in late life.

*Faith as Trust:* Faith as radical trust means that we ultimately rely on God to be our support and our safe place. Enns makes a clear case for prioritizing faith as trust over faith as correct belief in his book *The Sin of Certainty: Why God Desires Our Trust More than Our "Correct" Beliefs.* "This book is about thinking differently about faith, a faith that is not so much defined by *what* we believe but in *whom* we trust....I argue that we have misunderstood faith as a *what* word rather than a *who* word—as primarily *beliefs about* rather than primarily *as trust in.*"[11]

In Jesus's own prayer, we have a clear illustration of faith as trust. In the Garden of Gethsemane, he cried out, "Abba, Father, for you all things are possible; remove this cup from me; yet, not what I want, but what you want" (Mark 14:36–37) and on the cross, he uttered, "Father, into your hands I commend my spirit" (Luke 23:46). Both times, he accepted the bitter cup of his passion and death, with trust in a loving God who would bring good from evil, new life from death. *Abba* ("Papa") and *Amen* ("Let it be") are two words that most scripture scholars agree came from the very mouth of Jesus. The imagery of God as a loving "papa" or "daddy" suggests a relationship of intimacy, dependence, and protection; God is like a good parent who will take care of us, as good parents do with their young. Jesus modeled the trusting stance we are called to have in life, especially in the face of adversity.

*Aging and Faith*

Metaphors can make this aspect of faith come alive: faith is like floating in a deep ocean. If we thrash and flail about, we will eventually sink; but if we relax and trust, we will float. Matthew's story of Peter walking on the lake with Jesus is a figurative depiction of faith as trust. When he took his eyes off Jesus, he began to be afraid and started to sink (see Matt 14:22–33). Other biblical metaphors refer to God as our reliable rock and protective fortress—upholding and safeguarding us (see Ps 31). Denise Lavertov beautifully illustrates faith as trust in her poem "The Avowal."[12]

> As swimmers dare
> To lie face to the sky
> And water bears them,
> As hawks rest on air
> And air sustains them,
> So would I learn to attain
> Freefall, and float
> In Creator Spirit's deep embrace,
> Knowing no effort earns
> That all-surrounding grace.

Faith entails imitating trapeze artists who must learn to let go and to trust that they will be caught. "I can only fly freely when I know that there is a catcher to catch me," Henri Nouwen remarked in *Angels Over the Net*, a film about his trapeze theology. "If we take risks, to be free, in the air, in life, we have to know there's a catcher. We have to know that when we come down from it all, we're going to be caught, we're going to be safe....Trust the catcher."[13]

Trusting the catcher calls for a kind of not knowing or "blind trust." This kind of trust relates to the notion of "the dark night," when we have no tangible sense of God's presence and are called to rely on a hidden grace that will uphold us in our darkness and struggle. In her poem "Suspended," Levertov depicts what "blind trust" feels like:[14]

I had grasped God's garment in the void
But my hand slipped
On the rich silk of it.
The "everlasting arms"
my sister loved to remember
Must have upheld my leaden weight
From falling even so,
For though I claw at empty air and feel
Nothing, no embrace,
I have not plummeted.

"Trust is not marked by unflappable dogmatic certainty," Enns rightly observes, "but by embracing as a normal part of faith the steady line of mysteries and uncertainties that parade before our lives and seeing them as opportunities to trust more deeply."[15] If we consider faith as trust, its opposite is not doubt, but mistrust, worry, or anxiety. It is not surprising to hear people facing terminal illness say that they've been preparing for this their whole lives without knowing it. All the situations in life that have challenged them to let go and to trust God have trained them for dying, the biggest letting-go moment they have to face. These experiences have made trusting in God a habitual disposition that now strengthens them in their final hour of need.

*Faith as Our View of Reality*: Faith also relates to the way we perceive God and the whole of reality. Our image of God influences our religious experiences because we meet God as the one whom we imagine God to be. Paying attention to the way in which we image God and human life, therefore, is critically important for sound spiritual health and development. Borg presents three ways in which we can look at reality: as hostile, as indifferent, and as gracious. If we imagine life and God to be hostile, then our response to life is anxious, paranoid, and defensive. We must always be on the lookout for bad things to happen. If we imagine God to be indifferent to human purposes and ends, not caring about our concerns and aspirations, we are left having to rely on ourselves alone; help and support are not available elsewhere. In her *Dying: A Memoir*, Cory Taylor conveys this view of reality as indifferent. "What I've never believed is that God is watching over us, or has a personal interest in the state of our individual souls. In fact, if God exists at all, I think he/she must be a deity devoted to monumental indifference."[16] She explains that her religious instruction growing up was limited to knowing a few Bible stories from Sunday school. Put off by "their sanctimoniousness," she "preferred the darker tones of the Brothers Grimm, who presented a world where there was no redemption, where bad things happened for no reason, and nobody was punished. Even now I prefer that view of reality."[17]

The third way to view reality is to see it as life-giving and nourishing. God has brought all of us into existence and sustains us in life at every moment. In other words, reality is gracious, just as Jesus believed when he spoke about the birds in the air and the flowers in the field. God cares for all creatures, big and small. Furthermore, God loves everyone equally and causes the rain to fall on the just and unjust and the sun to shine on the good and the bad (see Matt 5:45–46). This view of reality grounds the possibility of radical trust. "It leads to the 'self-forgetfulness of faith' and thus to the ability to love and to be present to the moment."[18] Jesus urges us to view life as sustained by the generosity of divine grace. "Look at the birds of the air; they neither sow nor reap nor gather into barns, and yet your heavenly Father feeds them....Consider the lilies of the field, how they grow; they neither toil nor spin, yet I tell you, even Solomon in all his glory was not clothed like one of these" (Matt 6:26–29; see also Luke 12:22–34). "Consider the lilies," Emily Dickinson wrote to her cousins late in her life, "is the only commandment I ever obeyed."[19]

Faith—both as trust in the reliability of God and as a way of viewing life as sustained by divine graciousness—can play a significant role in our well-being as we age. Faith assures us that reality is ultimately gracious because the tender and caring love of God permeates everything. Teilhard de Chardin's "Prayer for the Grace to Age Well" reflects a spirituality that is grounded in faith. It also beautifully embodies the heart of Christian hope in the face of aging and dying.

> When the signs of age begin to mark my body
> (and still more when they touch my mind);
> when the ill that is to diminish me or carry me off
> strikes from without or is born within me;
> when the painful moment comes
> in which I suddenly awaken
> to the fact that I am ill or growing old;
> and above all at that last moment
> when I feel I am losing hold of myself
> and am absolutely passive within the hands
> of the great unknown forces that have formed me;
> in all those dark moments, O God,
> grant that I may understand that it is you
> (provided only my faith is strong enough)
> who are painfully parting the fibers of my being
> in order to penetrate to the very marrow
> of my substance and bear me away within yourself.[20]

# God Is Always More than We Can Imagine

Like Zen koans, biblical images of God's tender care of tiny sparrows and delicate lilies boggle our rational mind and strain our capacity to imagine a God who could care for each single person among the billions of people in the world. Such faith requires that we respect the utter transcendence of God, who is beyond human comprehension—always more than we can conceive in our mind and imagination. Believing that God is always greater counters our tendency to make God into our human image and likeness. Trusting faith requires the humble acknowledgment that God's power at work in us can do abundantly more than we can ask or imagine (Eph 3:20). Jesuit theologian Michael Buckley warns, "It is terribly misguided to set limits to the fulfillment of God's promises and providence or to fix boundaries to our confidence in his work in our lives. Human beings stammer as God approaches them....God—Utter Mystery—infinitely and pervasively present and at work in their lives."[21]

Speaking to our anxious hearts, Jesus tells us not to worry, but to trust because trust casts out fear and anxiety. Viewed as trust, faith clearly can contribute to aging well. Since we do not control all the variables that can impact our physical health and security—like strokes, cancer, and deteriorating bones or cognitive abilities—we naturally live with a certain amount of anxiety. Not knowing the turns our health will take, aging ushers in a host of anxiety-provoking concerns such as the following: What if I reach a point when I can no longer live at home on my own? What will I do? How will I deal with my loss of independence? If I need to make a decision about advance treatment, do I want to prolong my life as long as possible, no matter the cost, or do I want to forgo extraordinary treatment and enjoy the quality of life available, accepting a shortened life?

In dealing with the inevitable worries stirred by the unpredictable, faith as radical trust can help contain our anxieties and enable us to live more peacefully in the present. The Old Testament's account of the Israelites making a frantic escape from Egypt illustrates a sound strategy for dealing with the uncertainties of life. Soon after releasing the Israelites from captivity, the pharaoh suddenly changed his mind and sent his horsemen and chariots in hot pursuit of the fleeing Israelites. Feeling pinned between the fire-breathing Egyptians behind them and the wall of the sea in front of them, they panicked and complained to Moses: "Why did you lead us out of Egypt only to die in the wilderness? We told you that we would rather work for the Egyptians than die in the desert" (see Exod 14:11–12). In response, Moses told the people, "Do not be afraid, stand firm, and see the deliverance that the LORD will accomplish for you today....The LORD will fight for you, and you have only to keep still" (vv. 13–14). Then, in the very next verse, God said to Moses, "Tell the Israelites to go forward" (v. 15). These back-to-back verses seem to give conflicting orders. How could the people simultaneously keep still and keep moving? This, however, is only a seeming contradiction, because when Moses encouraged the people to keep still, he was not telling them to stop moving forward. Rather, he was encouraging them to still their anxious hearts—to trust in the saving power of God—and to keep moving ahead, one step at a time. While the Hebrew word used for *still* in Exodus 14:14 is not the same word translated "still" in Psalm 46:10, the spiritual point is the same: "Be still, and know that I am God!" This is sound advice for us today as we face the unknowns of the future and the randomness of life. Paradoxically, when we rely on the saving power of God, our own efforts will be more effective and less frantic, more hopeful and less desperate.

In practical terms, this biblical strategy to be still and still moving entails three steps. First, we begin by coping. Coping in the face of the unknown requires taking one day at a time and moving forward step by peaceful step. We cope successfully by staying grounded in the present and not being paralyzed by catastrophic expectations about what "could happen" in the future. This means avoiding the trap of "what if" thinking. Being obsessed with all the possible things that could go wrong is crazy making and paralyzing. Second, we try to cherish those most dear to us—our spouse, our children, our family and friends—and we try to be a bit more generous and gracious to those who cross our path. Third, we try to live each day with more immediacy and awareness, for example, delighting in, not rushing through, family dinners or savoring, not gulping down, a glass of full-bodied Burgundy. Living each day with greater awareness of the large and small blessings that we enjoy deepens our appreciation and gratitude for life. This threefold strategy encapsulates a practical approach to life as we strive to age gracefully. It enables us to heed the wisdom of this Chinese proverb: "That the birds of worry and care fly over your head, this you cannot change, but that they build nests in your hair, this you can prevent." We avoid excessive worry by dwelling in the "here and now" with awareness of all that the present situation offers.

# Faith Abets Graceful Aging

Faith can be a vital source of support when the challenges of aging make us weary and afraid. How can it not, if it grounds our lives in an enduring trust in God who promises to remain faithful to us throughout our life's journey? Christian faith does not deny the reality of pain and death. It does not say to us: "Fear not; trust in God who will see that none of the things you fear will happen to you." Instead, it reassures us that even if what we are afraid of does happen, we can trust that God will be with us. Though we walk through the valley of darkness, we fear no evil, because God, like a good shepherd, will protect us with his rod and staff.

Matthew's story of the three Magi reinforces the good news that God is present on our journey through life. The Magi experienced the abiding presence of God in several ways. God was present to them not only when they arrived at the cave in Bethlehem, but also in the stirring in their hearts that sent them off in search of the promised Messiah, in a guiding star that kept them on track, and in a dream that warned them of Herod's threat. During lonely nights far from home, they felt God's presence in their companionship and mutual encouragement to keep going when feeling discouraged. The unpredictable nature of aging can take us into unknown terrain far removed from the familiar and safe. Experiences like the sudden death of a loved one or the onset of a serious illness can disorient us and send us off searching for a new way of living. In such times of searching, faith can soothe our anxious hearts with the reassurance that, as with the three Magi, God accompanies us in more ways than we can imagine.

The disciples of Jesus were once given a dramatic lesson—meant also for us today—about how Christ is ever present. One day they were crossing the Lake of Galilee when a fierce storm enveloped their little boat. Frightened by the violent wind, the apostles were stricken with panic. Suddenly, Jesus appeared to them walking in the water. "It is I," he told them, "Do not be afraid" (John 6:20). Jesus then calmed the storm and the boat quickly came to shore.

This gospel story encourages us modern disciples to trust God when our fragile boat is rocked by waves of worry and torrents of trouble. At those times, we need to recognize how the risen Jesus is drawing near to us to still the storm. Calm will descend on us when we hear Jesus say, "Do not be afraid. It is I." The approach of the risen Jesus into our lives in stormy times is experienced mainly through people. After surgery to remove a malignant tumor in his brain, a friend of ours expressed his gratitude to his circle of friends: "We have found that God's love and healing are not add-ons: your support has been not only the sign of God's grace, but the principal way it has come to us....Your support helps open the windows for grace, which comes through many channels, the major one being friends, but also wonderful spouses, talented surgeons, radiologists with good aim, and insightful therapists."[22] To spot the presence of God in turbulent times, when we are jolted by the upheavals of life, however, is not easy, but requires us to "rummage" through our experience, the subject of the next chapter.

# SPIRITUAL EXERCISES AND PERSONAL REFLECTIONS

## A. Faith as Our Way of Perceiving God and Reality

"How does God feel about me?" If you were to ask yourself this question, what would be your spontaneous and honest response? How you think God feels about you is critically important because it greatly affects the way you feel about yourself and the kind of relationship you have with God. Discovering who we are in light of who God is, is perhaps the most important aspect of spiritual growth and transformation.

- Is God's love for us really unconditional in such a way that nothing can ever separate us from the love of God made visible in Christ (Rom 8:31–39), or is God's love for us conditional, capable of fluctuation based on our behavior and attitudes?
- Does God regard us with disappointment or delight?
- Does God's love for us depend on our performing in ways that gain God's approval or does God's love flow steadily into our lives, no matter what?

Your responses to these questions reflect the core of your faith.

## B. A Scriptural Reflection on God's Loving Care

Read the following verses from Matthew's Gospel:

Can you not buy two sparrows for a penny? And yet not one falls to the ground without your Father knowing.

Why, every hair on your head has been counted. So there is no need to be afraid.

(10:29–31; New Jerusalem Bible)

Dwell with the text, repeating a word, sentence, or phrase. Repetition allows the seed of God's word to sink into the inner soil of the soul.

- Pay attention to what in the passage catches your attention and glitters in your mind's eyes.
- What images are evoked within you?
- What feelings do these images stir up?

## C. Poetic Expressions of Faith as Trust

Read the two poems, "The Avowal" and "Suspended" by Denise Levertov, included in the chapter.

- How are they the same? How are they different?
- Play with the images; what do they stir up in you?
- Which describes your present experience of life?
- Which describes how you have been?
- With words or images, describe the experience that underlies each of the poems.

## D. Honoring How You Connect with the Sacred

Spirituality fosters faith by helping us pay attention to the life-giving Spirit that pervades all reality like a mysterious wind.

Read the following reflection and ask yourself how Spirit shows up in your life.

I am fascinated by the realm of Spirit. Art, literature, and music give access to it; mountains and oceans touch it, great trees and evocative waters whether surging or still; church liturgy, and prayer can touch it; stillness and silence give access to it—whatever speaks to our hearts and calls to the contemplative in each of us. Intimacy and relationships touch it. Augustine touched it when he said: "You have made us for yourself, O God, and our hearts can find no rest until they rest in you."[23]

# Chapter 2

# RUMMAGING FOR GOD IN TIMES OF CHALLENGE

God comes to you disguised as your life.

—Paula D'Arcy

"I will keep you safe on your journey." This was the divine promise given to Jacob when his life was in shambles. Following a family crisis precipitated by his own deceit, Jacob found himself far from home and suddenly alone as he fled from his brother Esau's murderous rage. In the darkness of night and in a sleep induced by fatigue, he encountered God and was fortified by God's promise of support as he faced an unknown future. "Wow, God was in this place and I did not know it." These were the first words that came from Jacob's mouth, as he awoke from a dream that reassured him that God would always be with him (see Gen 28:10–17). The promise God made to Jacob is also meant for us. This biblical story conveys a consoling message: no matter how life challenges us, God will be there to support us.

By the time we reach the afternoon of life, we have lived long enough to know that aging is not a smooth road but has its ups and downs. Like Jacob, we need to know that God is with us when rocky times leave us feeling vulnerable and afraid. While faith assures us of God's abiding presence, disruptive life events can disorient us and blur our perception. To find God in turbulent times may require some rummaging. Just like rummaging through a drawer looking for something we know is there but can't quite put our hands on, rummaging for God involves sorting through our experiences until we discover how God is present.

# Our Personal Story:
# Trusting God in Turbulent Times

In dealing with the twists and turns of our own journeys, we both, like Jacob, have felt supported by God, particularly when we faced life-changing transitions. Aging occurs gradually and many people mark its onset during midlife because this is when significant changes begin. Up to this point, most people are established in the style of life that launched their adult years and feel relatively secure. But gradually work may become less satisfying and relationships less fulfilling. Currents of discontent make us suddenly feel unmoored. "For years we have been comfortable in our work, clear in our relationships with others, settled in our spirituality. Then some part of this accustomed stability no longer 'works.' We begin to feel dislocated, disoriented. Negative feelings stir within us: embarrassment—what's wrong with me? Hurt—this is not fair; this should not be happening."[1] We find ourselves asking such questions as: Is this all there is? What do I really want from life? These questions take on some urgency because at midlife we find ourselves thinking about death—not only of our physical death but also the death of our youthful dreams and illusions. The brevity of life dawns on us and we realize that we are given only a limited time to live out our dreams and desires. No longer can we cling to our childhood illusion of the future as an indefinite horizon—unending like the mountains on a Chinese scroll.

At late midlife, about twenty-five years ago, we both experienced a crisis in our religious vocation. Each of us was living a very different life than the one we are today. Today we are "formers"—Wilkie, a former Jesuit priest, and Noreen, a former Sister of St. Joseph of Carondelet. The question of how we arrived at where we are defies a short and simple answer, but in looking back, we know without a doubt that it was faith that guided and sustained us during that time of upheaval and disorientation. To some of our family and friends, that we would risk leaving the security of religious life at age fifty was incomprehensible. But Noreen's diagnosis of breast cancer forced her to look more earnestly at the increasing unrest she had been feeling and to face her questions about whether continuing to live as a nun would be life-giving as she entered the second half of life. What was the unrest about? Where was God in this midlife crisis of health and vocation? After thirty-two years, could God be leading her to another way of life?

Wilkie's vocation crisis began with feelings of discontentment and mild depression. What, he wondered, was underlying his sudden unease in living as a Jesuit priest? As he struggled to understand his feelings, he had a dream that caused him to reevaluate his vocation. And over the next few years, with the help of a spiritual director and a counselor, he came to a peaceful decision to leave the Jesuits.

# Awareness and Discernment

To deal effectively with any life crisis, we need to pay attention to what we are feeling and ask ourselves what the feelings are telling us. What is causing this upheaval? What in our life is no longer sustaining? Facing, rather than denying, that we are in crisis moves us into a liminal space, a time of not knowing, when we feel suspended in midair and must trust that God is with us. Patient endurance and the willingness to live with uncertainty are necessary if we are to find out where God is leading us. Efforts we make to avoid facing the questions and the upheaval they cause may work for a while. Numbing ourselves with alcohol, drugs, overwork, or an affair may temporarily ease our pain and discomfort, but only for so long. What we need most at times of crises is awareness. According to Gestalt therapy, awareness leads to greater "response-ability" and expands our options and possibilities. Along with awareness, we need the courage to make whatever changes are necessary, even when those changes entail the loss of security, status, or comfort. Change, even when we choose it for the sake of our own well-being, is a risk. There are no guarantees. We can be courageous in times of radical change only if we have a lively faith in God's loving presence, a faith that "sustains our confidence that a crisis is not the punishment of a vindictive God but the intrusion of a God who leads us down strange paths toward new life."[2]

When we think about the full life we presently enjoy—more than twenty years of marriage, a circle of close friends, and meaningful work—we are deeply grateful for God's support on our journey. Leaving religious life was a leap of faith into deep, unknown waters. Remembering Peter, who sank when he doubted, we faced waves of worry—where to live, how to earn a living, how to save for the future—with trust that God would keep us afloat. As we look back, we recognize clear moments of grace when we felt held and enabled by God to "freefall, and float in Creator Spirit's deep embrace."

# A Cancer-Caused Crisis

More recently, I (Wilkie) faced a new crisis; this time it was cancer that upended my life. While my vocation crisis had unfolded gradually over a period of several years, my health crisis literally happened overnight. On the Wednesday of Holy Week 2016, I was awakened by a sharp pain under my left eye, and within hours my left cheek and upper lip were numb. Two days later, a malignant tumor was discovered in my left sinus cavity and I was scheduled for a biopsy that would determine what kind of cancer I was dealing with. And after a grueling nine-day wait for the pathology report, I learned that I had stage one lymphoma. Six rounds of chemotherapy followed, transporting me into a "cloud of unknowing," where any clarity I might have had—about what God was about in my life and what was in store for my future—quickly blurred into darkness. Those nine days of waiting were among the darkest of my life; they were definitely the longest! Being diagnosed with cancer was a "difficult grace": difficult because it was frightening and disruptive; a grace because rummaging through cancer helped me discover how richly present God is in my life. With Jacob, I discovered that "God was in this place, but I did not know it."

# Faith: God's Way to Us on God's Terms

Cancer posed a serious challenge to my faith: How do I make sense of this sudden intrusion of a life-threating illness? In this dark place, I read something that illumined my path forward. "Faith is not the way to God on our terms, it is the way of God to us on his [*sic*] terms," writes Eugene Peterson in his book on the Jesus way.[3] These words triggered in me what psychologists call a gestalt shift, when one's perception suddenly changes. Faith—seen as God's approach into my life—helped me to reframe the onset of cancer and to move ahead without being dragged down by discouragement. My bout with cancer was not to be lamented as an unwanted interruption, but rather to be embraced as the graceful main event—

the way that God was approaching me on God's terms! Instead of focusing on God's absence, I needed to pay closer attention to God's advent. Without denying the darkness of a cancer diagnosis, I was called to rummage in the darkness—in order to find how God would enter my life in a more intimate way. Instead of bemoaning my situation, I needed to value my illness as an opportunity to encounter the mysterious presence of God. An opportunity to grow in faith, "trusting obediently in what we cannot control, living in obedient relationship to the One we cannot see, venturing obediently into a land that we know nothing about."[4] My challenge entailed an ongoing discernment of how God was drawing near.

# Rummaging for God in Our Inner World

Even with this shift to a positive spiritual outlook, living with cancer was still a struggle. As I waited for a final diagnosis, my prayer was a jumble of emotions. Inner voices clamored with their conflicting advice: one voice counseled me to accept cancer as the present condition for God's coming into my life; another voice, a bit more rebellious, advocated resisting it as a painful misfortune. One morning while praying, I monitored the various inner voices and was surprised by what I heard. At first, there was a voice that cried out, "Why me? This isn't fair." This voice was one of angry protest and sad lament, washed in self-pity. Next followed a voice that said, "Why not me? Do you think you're exempt from the human condition and can escape the suffering that afflicts so many in the world?" This voice led me to accept my illness and made me feel more compassionate toward all those who suffer sickness and pain. Then, to my surprise, I again heard a voice saying, "Why me?" But this time, the "Why me?" voice was not angry, but grateful. This "Why me?" opened up an extended review of all the blessings and advantages I have been given: a happy childhood growing up in Honolulu; thirty-two satisfying years living as a Jesuit in the company of good, intelligent, and dedicated men; and now twenty years of a joyful married life. I have so much to be grateful for!

When we pay attention to our inner life, we hear various voices, like an inner conversation between different aspects of ourselves; not auditory hallucination, but interior psychic states, what Ignatius of Loyola, in medieval language, referred to as "spirits." Some of these voices are "good spirits"—enlivening and creative; others are "bad spirits"—stifling and destructive. Good spirits lead us to consolation (feelings of peace, love, joy, hope) and a felt sense of God's presence. Bad spirits lead us to desolation (feelings of sadness, agitation, discouragement, hopelessness) and a feeling of God's absence. Identifying these inner voices and choosing which to follow is what Ignatian spirituality calls "the discernment of spirits." It is important to pay attention to the inner voices that compete for influence over us, for reasons the following story illustrates: One day a disciple approached his guru and reported, "I feel like there are two dogs in me fighting all day long. One is good and kind, the other is bad and mean." "Which one wins?" asks the guru. "The one I feed more," answered the disciple. Spiritual growth entails being aware of competing inner voices and choosing which of them we want to hold sway over our thoughts and actions.

# Inner Conflict Revealed in a Dream

Monitoring the conflicting inner voices within kept me aware of my struggles and enabled me to share my honest feelings in prayer. A dream also shed light on my divided self and the warring parts within me. I wrote this dream in my journal.

*The Dream:* Two friends of mine are pushing against each other in a fighting match. The fighting quickly escalates and one of them picks up a crucifix and smashes the other on the head.

***My Interpretation:*** The dream reveals an inner conflict, one part fighting another. Looking at my associations with the two dream figures, I associate the one figure with a pacifist Quaker, who surrenders to reality in quiet serenity. I associate the opposing figure with someone who is angry at an aspect of his life and holds a grudge against God for allowing it to exist. This dream lays bare my inner conflict between accepting my cancer in a faith-filled way and angrily protesting it as unfair. While I have experienced moments of lamenting and complaining, my response, for the most part, has been one of trustful acceptance—believing that somehow my cancer can usher in a deeper entrance of God into my life.

The dream is also warning me that I need to acknowledge the protesting part of me as a natural human response, not spiritualize it away. The angry dream figure who smashes the other with a crucifix is a part of me that I need to own. This angry, self-pitying part of me surfaces when I notice others feeling full of life and energy—not suffering like me—and I feel envious; it also shows up on days when I am tired of feeling sick and debilitated. I recognize this as a natural, human emotion. Yet in terms of the discernment of spirits, I also recognize it as a "bad spirit" that leads to desolation and discontent. Thus, I choose not to let this "spirit" or inner psychic state hold sway. I choose rather to let the spirit of trusting acceptance draw me into a greater awareness of God in my experience of cancer and the debilitating side effects of chemotherapy.

# Cancer as a Spiritual Experience

My experience of cancer—now in remission and requiring regular checkups with my oncologist—has been spiritually fruitful in several ways. Learning to trust God deeply is a life-long process, yet cancer was a crash course in becoming more trusting and less controlling, more willing and less willful. A passage from John's Gospel framed my cancer experience in a meaningful way. In an intimate conversation with Jesus, Peter, who had just expressed his love for Jesus three times, was told,

> Very truly, I tell you, when you were younger, you used to fasten your own belt and to go wherever you wished. But when you grow old, you will stretch out your hands, and someone else will fasten a belt around you and take you where you do not wish to go. (John 21:18)

After saying this, Jesus said to Peter, "Follow me." This text spoke to my heart, inspiring me to trust in the mysterious lead of God, as I felt "belted" by cancer at age seventy-two. As we face all the unknown contingencies of old age, peace comes when we can go with the flow of God's lead in the unfolding of our lives.

In my struggle with cancer, I, like the anxious disciples being tossed by fierce winds as they crossed the lake, sensed the consoling presence of the risen Jesus, reassuring me: "Peace, do not be afraid; it is I." This instilled a steady stream of peace throughout the turbulent months of numerous biopsies and long chemo treatments. While having a serious illness like cancer was not the way I would have chosen to grow closer to God, I was led to believe that this was the path being laid out for me. This insight was a gift that I received in prayer, not something I imposed on my experience in an effort to deny my pain. Like the two disciples on the way to Emmaus—weighted down with sadness and dashed hopes—I felt consoled by the risen Jesus who also accompanies us on our journey today. Perhaps I was predisposed to receive this grace by Ignatius of Loyola, who encourages us when contemplating the resurrection to "consider the office of consoler that Christ our Lord exercises, and compare it with the way in which friends are wont to console each other" (*Spiritual Exercises*, 224).

Finally, I realize more than ever that the approach of God into my life is not an esoteric thing, but comes mainly through people: Noreen, family, friends, neighbors, and those I minister to in spiritual direction. Emails, cards, telephone calls, gifts of flowers and food were touching embodiments of love and a strong reminder of how "Christ plays in ten thousand places, lovely in limbs and lovely in eyes not his to the Father through the features of men's [*sic*] faces."[5]

# The Holy Ground of Our Experience

To age gracefully requires that we cultivate our ability to pay attention to the holy ground of our experience and to rummage for God in everyday events—not just in painful ones, but in *all* our experiences. One day Moses was tending his flock in the wilderness and came to Horeb, the mountain of God. There Moses saw a flame of fire coming from the middle of a bush. While the bush was aflame, it was not burning up. Drawn by curiosity, Moses approached the bush. As he drew closer, he heard God call to him from the middle of the bush: "Moses, Moses....Come no closer! Remove the sandals from your feet, for the place on which you are standing is holy ground....I am the God of your father" (Exod 3:4–6). Moses's encounter with God before the burning bush reminds us that our life experiences are where we encounter God. Common occurrences in daily life can disclose God's presence if we look at our God-soaked world with prayerful attention. With eyes of faith, any bush can be a burning bush revelatory of God.

To rummage for God in the rush and routine of daily experience requires a contemplative stance that keeps us awake and fresh in our perceptions of people and events and open to being surprised, not jaded or cynical. This contemplative stance will enable us to notice the living God who comes to us "disguised as our life." Like Moses, who heard God call his name while in the wilderness, we too can have a personal encounter with the living God and find support in the wilderness of our lives. A vibrant faith is experience based and not just dependent on what we have been taught by others. If faith is to be a support to aging well, merely belonging to a religion is no longer sufficient. Personal spiritual experience is required to maintain a vital faith. Jesuit Karl Rahner, one of the leading Catholic theologians of the twentieth century, put it starkly, "The Christian of the future will either be a mystic, one who has experienced something, or he will cease to be anything at all."[6] According to him, lively faith requires a firsthand, personal connection with the Sacred. Not referring to otherworldly experiences, he was thinking of a "mysticism of daily life," which enables ordinary Christians to spot the movements of God's Spirit in the encounters of daily life. By "mysticism," Rahner was clearly not referring to parapsychological or extraordinary experiences of the Sacred, but to experiences in ordinary life when we have caught a glimmer of God in events of

- love and beauty,
- wonder and awe,
- understanding and acceptance,
- forgiveness and reconciliation,
- kindness and generosity,
- hurt and healing.

Celtic spirituality labels these moments as "thin places" where the fine veil between human life and the divine presence that envelops all reality drops, revealing the mysterious presence of the Holy One in our midst. Experiences like these are graced reminders that "earth's crammed with heaven." Thus, Rahner encourages us to develop our mystical potential and to foster a faith that can illuminate reality in such a way that the sustaining presence of God shines forth. As we grow in our ability to notice intimations of the Sacred in a world drenched in divinity, a solid personal faith will emerge. It is this kind of personal faith that supports aging with grace.

# Experiencing God in Both Light and Darkness

In rummaging for God's presence in our lives, we naturally turn to positive experiences of peace and love, wonder and joy. We identify "God moments" as times of consolation, when we experience God's love and are able to let go and trust God. While affirming these moments as tangible experiences of God's self-communication, Rahner also directs our attention to difficult and dark times. He suggests that God can also be experienced at the time in life when "everyday realities break and dissolve," when we struggle with meaning at work, betrayal in relationships, dryness in prayer, and disillusionment with authority.[7] At such times, we may experience the Divine Presence as a surprising ability to endure and to hope in the face of hardship and opposition. In some unfathomable way, we discover a Source of strength that goes beyond anything we can attribute to ourselves. Rahner points to this sustaining Source as the mysterious presence of the God of Light, upholding us in our dark night. "Weakness…is the night in which [God]…appears— not always as felt reassurance, but more often as a hidden power to continue, faithful even when one does not feel the strength, even when fidelity means simply putting one foot in front of the other."[8]

In an excerpted piece from her book, published in *Luminos: Faith and Light for the Journey*, Becky Garrison recounts her experience of this God of Darkness. Fittingly, the piece is entitled "Where is God?" Growing up with alcoholic parents, she describes her painful childhood.

> Over time my parents slowly started to lose little pieces of themselves. As they got worse, the shame of my family's demise drove my extended family and all their friends to seek higher ground, leaving us black sheep to forage for ourselves. Bit by bit they started to go. I don't

> know at what point my parents' souls actually left their
> bodies, after which, I pray, they were welcomed into
> God's loving arms. But it was pretty clear that by the
> time we buried them, there was nothing left.[9]

Struggling with the darkness of her dysfunctional childhood, she anguished over God's inscrutable ways: "Why did God seem to take a dirt nap as I buried my father and mother within an eleven-month period? This isn't how a sixteen-year-old's life is supposed to go." In an attempt to console her and her siblings, the priest who officiated at her father's funeral reassured them. "Even though your father couldn't help himself, he was there for countless others who were lost," he told them. "I've been getting calls for hours from people saying how much the reverent Dr. Karl Claudius Garrison Jr. changed their lives," he added. Then at the funeral, he reminded them of the "obligation to keep on living and loving and dying." At the time, the priest's words provided not "one lick of spiritual solace." Yet those words stuck with her and made her wonder if God's light had not mysteriously slipped into her dark experiences.

> The words by some priest I only met once and didn't
> care for one whit (mild understatement) said something
> that enabled me to hang on to life, like some demented,
> rabid pit bull. In hindsight, I can see the hand of God
> working through this unknown priest and a few kind
> souls. Their words entered into me like the tiny specks
> of sunlight, illuminating what otherwise was a dark,
> cavernous pit that stank to high heaven.[10]

"For reasons I cannot explain," she shares, "my teenage blues never morphed into clinical depression or worse. I survived the loss of a close friend who committed suicide during my senior year of college." Garrison's story attests to the truth of Rahner's insight that God can be experienced in darkness, as well as in light—

encouraging for all of us who are committed to rummaging for God as we age!

# Rummaging in Retrospect

Recalling past times when we have experienced God's help can be an important way of rummaging for God in the present. It can expand our capacity to trust that God is still with us today—even though we might not feel it at the moment. When feeling abandoned, hindsight can clarify how God's faithful presence has been with us all along. Once, Moses said to God,

> "Show me your glory, I pray." And [God] said, "I will make all my goodness pass before you, and will proclaim before you the name, 'The LORD'; and I will be gracious to whom I will be gracious, and will show mercy on whom I will show mercy. But," he said, "you cannot see my face; for no one shall see me and live." And the LORD continued, "See, there is a place by me where you shall stand on the rock; and while my glory passes by I will put you in a cleft of the rock, and I will cover you with my hand until I have passed by; then I will take away my hand, and you shall see my back; but my face shall not be seen." (Exod 33:18–23).

The Hebrew word *achorai*, translated as God's "back" in this passage, would be more spiritually insightful if translated as God's "afterwards," for it is often later, after God has passed by, that we recognize how the glory of God has graced our lives.[11] The popular reflection "Footprints" reflects this biblical truth.

> One night a man had a dream. He dreamed he was walking along the beach with the Lord. Across the sky flashed

scenes from his life. For each scene, he noticed two sets of footprints in the sand: one belonging to him, and the other to the Lord.

When the last scene of his life flashed before him, he looked back at the footprints in the sand. He noticed that many times along the path of his life there was only one set of footprints. He also noticed that it happened at the very lowest and saddest times in his life.

This really bothered him and he questioned the Lord about it. "Lord, you said that once I decided to follow you, you'd walk with me all the way. But I have noticed that during the most troublesome times in my life, there is only one set of footprints. I don't understand why when I needed you most you would leave me."

The Lord replied, "My child, my precious child, I love you and I would never leave you. During your times of trial and suffering, when you see only one set of footprints, it was then that I carried you."

*—Unknown*

Thus the mystery of the disappearing footprints is solved. This consoling insight, however, may come only in retrospect, when our eyes are opened to see God's "afterwards." With patience, we are called to hold in memory dark experiences of the past until grace gradually illuminates how God has always been in those painful times; with this realization can come much consolation and healing. Memory serves us well when it makes us mindful of the enduring presence of a God who promises to walk always with us.

# SPIRITUAL EXERCISES AND PERSONAL REFLECTIONS

## A. Finding God at Home

Rummaging for God as a regular practice of mindfulness can cultivate our ability to find God at home. God is "at home" in the sense that God is ever present and available, as well as in the sense that God can be found at home, where we live. A rabbinical story expresses well the truth that God is to be encountered where God has placed us, not in a heavenly city or special place.[12]

In the hiddenness of time there was a poor man who left his village, weary of his life, longing for a place where he could escape all the struggles of this earth. He set out in search of a magical city—the heavenly city of his dreams, where all things would be perfect. He walked all day and by dusk found himself in a forest, where he decided to spend the night. Eating the crust of bread he had brought, he said his prayers and, just before going to sleep, placed his shoes in the center of the path, pointing them in the direction he would continue the next morning. Little did he imagine that while he slept, a practical joker would come along and turn his shoes around, pointing them back in the direction from which he had come.

The next morning, in all the innocence of folly, he got up, gave thanks to the Lord of the Universe, and started on his way again in the direction that his shoes pointed. For a second time he walked all day, and toward evening finally saw the magical city in the distance. It wasn't as large as he had expected. As he got closer, it looked curiously familiar. But he pressed on, found a street much

31

like his own, knocked on a familiar door, greeted the family he found there—and lived happily ever after in the magical city of his dreams.

Faith does not transport us to a magical city but enables us to appreciate anew the rich blessings that are contained at home, in the ordinary circumstances of daily life.

# B. Finding God in All Things

Writing in her journal, a woman expresses with poetic beauty the Ignatian vision that everything not only comes from God as gift, but that God dwells intimately in all that exists (*Spiritual Exercises*, 234–5):

God is the rain that pours down to nourish the earth, and the rainbow arched across the sky after the rain.

God is the bud beginning to sprout from the soil and the centuries-old Sequoia tree pointing toward the endless sky.

God is the waterfall, overflowing with life and love, pouring it out for me beautifully and powerfully.

God is the sparkle in my eye, the story behind my smile, the melody in my laughter, and the spring in my step.

God is the outstretched hand, the warm embrace, the pat on the back, the stroking of my hair, the warmth of the sun on my skin.

God is the knowing, the not knowing, and the wanting to know.

God is passion, freedom, truth, beauty, and love.

God is a kind word on a rough day and a letter from a loved one far away.

God is the familiarity of the now and the uncertainty of the future.

God is home.

God is the friend who is always there for me, who challenges me, believes in me, and loves me fully for me.

God is the lucky break that I don't quite deserve but am thankful for anyway.

God is food on the table, a new day of life, water for a shower, clothes to wear, books to read, and a bed to sleep in.

God is learning and teaching, running, playing, singing, and dancing.

God is friendship and a surprise phone call.

God is riding in the car with the windows down, wind in my hair, singing to the radio.

God is the person I struggle to accept, struggle to love, and struggle to appreciate.

God is the part of me that I struggle to accept, struggle to love, and struggle to appreciate.

God is the pieces that seem to fall into place, and those that fall out of place and make me search for a better way.

God is the lesson in mistakes and the wisdom in trials.

God is the letting go, the deepest desire.

God is my talents and gifts, my hands, my feet, my voice, calling me to action—to serve, to live out God's dream for me and the world.

God is the dreamer and the dream, the lover, the beloved, the love.[13]

# Chapter 3

# ACHES AND PAINS

## The New Normal

You know you are getting older, when your back
goes out more than you do!

—Anonymous

We can complain because rose bushes have
thorns, or rejoice because thorn bushes have roses.

—Abraham Lincoln

Aging compels us to accept aches and pains as the new normal. As
a doctor assured a man in his seventies, "All my patients your age
who are free of aches are dead." Bodily health varies greatly among
individuals due to genetic factors, the quality of medical care,
dietary habits, and environmental conditions. Nevertheless, a time
comes for all of us when our bodies register the wear and tear of
use and we begin to experience the inevitable physical discomforts
that come with age—muscle aches, strained joints, arthritic hips
and knees. One geriatric specialist, who has conducted more than

a hundred studies on aging, when asked if there is any predictable pathway to aging, answered, "No, we just fall apart."[1]

# Physical Pain Is Inevitable; Suffering Is an Option

Accepting physical pain as a natural part of growing old enables us to age gracefully. It requires that we not allow pain to diminish us or to spoil our appreciation and enjoyment of life. "Each of us will find his or her own path to this acceptance—some through humor, others through sharing, still others through conscious spiritual practice—but whatever the means that allow us to live in our aging bodies with grace, rather than anger, morbidity, or denial," Ram Dass wisely states, "it is crucial that we find them."[2]

Physical pain, however, is not the same as suffering. Physical pain originates in our bodies, but suffering as a response to pain is created by our mind. We are referring here to pain as a physical sensation, though in ordinary speech the word *pain* is also used to describe unpleasant emotional states like disappointment or grief. Suffering comes when we respond negatively to physical pain and complain that this should not be happening to us: "It's not fair! Why me? I should not be in pain like this! It's a drag on my life and what I want to be doing!" Such negative thinking has the capacity to make us miserable. Frustration, anger, sadness, depression, hopelessness, impatience, and anxiety are natural outcomes of such a response to pain. Suffering occurs when we complain and resist our reality because it does not conform to our desires. While physical pain is inevitable, this kind of suffering is optional.

The story of Scott Hamilton, winner of the 1984 Olympic gold medal in men's figure skating, illustrates how our response to painful health conditions shapes our emotional state. After overcoming stage 4 testicular cancer in 1997, he learned in 2004 that he had a pituitary tumor, one that had wrapped itself around his optic nerve. While benign, the tumor, he feared, could dangerously crowd his brain. He prayed fervently that the tumor would disappear. And after radiation, the tumor did go away—only to reappear in 2010. Surgery, however, resulted in an aneurysm that temporarily blinded him in one eye. During this severe health crisis, his wife, Tracie, said to him in a pep talk, "Joy is not the lack of suffering or fear, it's how we choose to handle the suffering and fear." Her words resonated so deeply that when the tumor made its third appearance in 2016, Hamilton's response was different from before. This time there was no "why me?" "I figured I needed to go through this with joy," he shared. "It was just a muscle I need to build, like the muscles I built skating."[3]

Psychologist Victor Frankl's *Man's Search for Meaning* illustrates valuable truths on dealing with pain. Observing fellow prisoners in a Nazi concentration camp, Frankl concluded that having a sense of meaning makes all the difference in how pain affects us. He noticed that those prisoners who persevered had a purpose for clinging to survival—like a loved one to live for, a manuscript or novel to complete, or some life project to finish. Having a *why* to live enabled them to bear almost any *how*. Meaning sustained their endurance. In contrast, those who languished and succumbed seemed unable to envision a meaning for living that could help them push through the pain with the hope of someday being liberated. Frankl believed that there is a space between stimulus and response, and in that space is our power to choose our response. Our serenity hangs on the choice we make.

Two important truths for gracious aging emerge from Frankl's observations: first, we *can choose* how to respond to painful situations; and second, pain loses its ability to drag us down when we perceive that it has some meaning and purpose. A classic example is a woman undergoing the pains of labor and childbirth, knowing that it will issue forth in new life. We can more easily accept the pain that comes with such experiences as childbirth, surgery, and chemotherapy, for example, when we keep our eyes on the hopeful outcome they offer.

Shortly before turning fifty-one, Episcopal priest Cricket Cooper was diagnosed with non-Hodgkin's lymphoma and suddenly found her life turned upside down. She struggled with how to integrate cancer into her life in a meaningful way. What came to her was to frame her eighteen weeks of painful chemo treatment as a spiritual pilgrimage. With each round of chemotherapy, she travelled to a different pilgrimage site. Viewing her bout with cancer as a spiritual pilgrimage helped her to contain the wild swings, the anxious ups and downs, of treatment.[4] "This is the pilgrim's path—not the need for everything to be perfect, but the deep desire to experience everything as it happens....I was learning imperfectly, not to label events or thoughts as 'good' or 'bad.' I was discovering how to live my life with gentleness, curiosity, and vulnerability."[5] She tried to adhere to the Buddhist teaching that to end suffering, we have to attune ourselves to the present moment—its joys and pain—without labeling our experience as either good or bad. We need to observe both our joyful and painful moments equally without attachment. Similarly, to view late life as a spiritual pilgrimage can be a positive way of dealing with the unexpected twists and turns of this final leg of our journey. Unlike a tourist who expects to be entertained, a pilgrim hopes to be graced. Pilgrimage is a hopeful image because those who set forth on a pilgrimage expect to find God with them all along the way—as well as at the journey's end.

The Buddhist path to removing the sting of suffering through a broad acceptance of all that life brings—without labeling our experience as good or bad—resonates with Christian wisdom. For instance, the "Welcoming Prayer,"[6] a favorite of those who practice centering prayer, offers a means to cultivate a serene way of embracing reality, even when it does not conform to our desires.

Gently become aware of your body
And your interior state.

# AGING WITH WISDOM AND GRACE

Welcome, welcome, welcome,
I welcome everything that comes to
Me in the moment
Because I know it is for my healing.
I welcome all thoughts,
Feelings, emotions, persons,
Situations and conditions.

I let go of my desire for security.

I let go of my desire for approval.

I let go of my desire for control.

I let go of my desire to change any
Situation, condition,
Person,
Or myself.

I open to the
Love and presence of God
And
The healing action and grace within.

Richard Rohr offers another Christian formulation of what he also calls "The Welcoming Prayer." According to him, "Forgiving reality for being what it is" enables us not to "lose presence in the moment." To achieve a nonevaluative openness to all our experience, he recommends the following:

First, identify a hurt or an offense in your life. Remember the feelings you first experienced with this hurt and feel them the way you first felt them. Notice how this shows up in your body. Paying attention to your body's sensations keeps you from jumping into the mind and its dualistic games of good guy/bad guy, win/lose, either/or.

After you can identify the hurt and feel it in your body, welcome it. Stop fighting it. Stop splitting and blaming. Welcome the grief. Welcome the anger. It's hard to do, but for some reason, when we name it, feel it, and welcome it, transformation can begin.[7]

From a Jewish perspective, a Talmudic story about a certain Rabbi Akiba illustrates well this kind of willingness to experience everything as it happens without being attached to a particular outcome.

In the turbulent first century, the rabbi once traveled in a strange country where mystery still dwelt. He had taken with him three possessions—an ass, a rooster, and a lamp—and had stopped at night in a village where he hoped to find lodging. When the people there drove him out, he was forced to spend the night in a forest nearby. But Rabbi Akiba bore all pains with ease, being heard always to say, "All that God does is done well." So he found a tree under which to stop, lit his lamp, and prepared to study Torah briefly before going to sleep. But a fierce wind suddenly blew out the flame, leaving him with no choice but to rest. Later that night wild animals came through and chased away his rooster. Still later, thieves passed by and took his ass. Yet in each case, Rabbi Akiba simply responded by saying, "All that God does is done well."

The next morning, he returned to the village where he had stopped the night before, only to learn that enemy soldiers had come by in the night, killing everyone in their beds. Had he been permitted to stay there, he too would have died. He learned also that the raiding army had traveled through the same part of the forest where he had slept. If they had seen the light of his lamp, if the rooster had crowed, or if the ass had brayed, again he would have been killed. And how did Rabbi Akiba respond? He simply replied as he always did, "All that God does is done well."[8]

There is a universal ring of truth when different faith traditions come to the same conclusion about the best stance to take toward life's ups and downs.

# "Growing Pains" in Later Life

It might sound a bit strange to talk about "growing pains" in our elder years. Growing pains are usually associated with an awkward stage of life, like puberty or the insecurity of leaving home for the first time or the discomfort of starting a new job. At such times, we willingly endured the painful unease because there is meaning and purpose in it. Is it possible to consider that the pain and difficulties we experience in later life are also growing pains? Both developmental psychology and Christian spirituality view late life as a time that is ripe with possibility for a degree of growth in maturity and wisdom that can only come with advanced age and life experience. Both teach that growth and transformation are ongoing and lifelong, and when we stay open to life's often painful challenges, we can be more tomorrow than we are today.

The inevitability of aches and pains as we get older motivates us to look at the possibility for growth that they offer.

*Pain can fashion a compassionate heart more sensitive to the sufferings of others.* An inescapable aspect of human life, pain can either separate or connect us to others. It can isolate us in a prison of self-absorption or it can provide an experiential basis for connecting with others who also experience pain, like, perhaps, those who sit near us in the doctor's waiting room, anxious as we are to be treated. When we empathize with the pain of others, the borders of our hearts are extended to take in—even for just a moment—the painful plight of others near and far. We might, for example, be better able to feel compassion for the poor of the world, who lack adequate medical care and the pain relief that we take for granted. "When we cease to resist our grief," writes Ram Dass, "we learn that, painful as it may be, grief is an integral part of elder wisdom, a force that humbles and deepens our hearts, connects us to the grief of the world, and enables us to be of help."[9]

Just as the pain of grief or illness can connect us to others, they can also separate us, if we hide our sickness out of embarrassment. A story that Cricket Cooper tells about herself delightfully illustrates this. One day during her cancer treatment, she was vesting for a healing service at the cathedral and became self-conscious about her physical appearance.

> While the good folks waited in their seats for the service to start, I was hiding in the vesting room, nervously adjusting the wig, and trying to hang the bag on my body [she had to wear a drug pump satchel] so I didn't yank the IV cord from my chest and didn't have a bizarre bulge appearing from under my robes.
>
> It's funny how we judge ourselves. Nobody was going to care whether my robes hung symmetrical or not. Why was I whipping myself into such a tizzy?

As she began the healing service, this is what unfolded:

> As if rehearsed, a guy in the front row pulled up his t-shirt and said, "Hey, I have an implant insulin pump!" Across the aisle, another guy pulled up the leg of his shorts and said, "I've got a bladder bag strapped to my leg!" A woman behind him yanked down her top to

show us her heart valve scar. It happed so fast, and they were all beaming like first-graders at a show-and-tell.[10]

This experience brought home an important realization: "Now my illness was on full display, and the only person who was incapable of looking at my woundedness was me." Later on, she described the healing grace of discovering "that the things we are most afraid of, which seem like they separate us from others, are precisely the things that bring us closer together."

By connecting us to others in our common humanity, pain contributes to both our human and spiritual growth. In the 1960s, psychologist Abraham Maslow triggered a paradigm shift in personality studies—a change of focus from studying pathological personalities to observing people who thrived in their life and work. He discovered that these "self-actualizing" persons felt deeply united with others in a worldwide familyhood and identified with them as brothers and sisters with similar trials and tribulations as their own. Spiritually, when pain deepens our empathy and compassion for others, it moves us closer to loving inclusively as God does.

*Pain can make us humble and more able to acknowledge that we need others.* As a Christian virtue, humility is a peaceful acceptance of our place in the universe and a grateful acknowledgment that we rely totally on God. Everything we enjoy—breath and bread alike—is a gift from God. Human limitation need not be a source of shame, since it does not point to any deficiency in us, but rather reflects our nature as creatures and links us to God in intimate and grateful dependence.

Admitting our dependency on God does not diminish our human dignity. The stalwart fishermen of Gloucester, Massachusetts, who regularly brave fierce Atlantic storms, state their need for God in a simple prayer: "Dear God, help us for we are just tiny boats in a huge sea." Even famous leaders are unashamed to confess their need of God's help. It is told that Admiral Hyman Rickover, the father of the atomic submarine, gave a plaque inscribed with the Fisherman's Prayer to President John F. Kennedy, who placed it prominently in the Oval Office. This prayer captures how inadequate we sometimes feel in a world that is not altogether safe, predictable, and friendly. In Jesus's eyes, those who acknowledge their dependence on God are blessed, for they are "poor in spirit."

Learning to be humble takes a lifetime. Ego dies a slow death and can angrily resist the limitations brought on by physical diminishment. Our ego protests, "I'd rather do it myself! I don't feel good depending on others!" Our pride resists the growing dependence on others that often accompanies aging. When we are incapacitated by illness and pain, however, we are given the opportunity to grow in humble acceptance of our limitations and to be grateful to those who help us in our weakness.

*Pain makes us vulnerable and opens us up to receiving love.* Vulnerability is not something we naturally desire. In fact, we spend so much of our adult life securing ourselves in the world in order to protect ourselves from being vulnerable. We want to be strong and independent. While being able to stand on our own two feet is an important task of adult development, fierce independence can be an obstacle to relationships. Personal autonomy ceases to be a value when it impedes relationships and community, whereas vulnerability opens the door to greater intimacy and sharing. While vulnerability is an abiding condition of human life, we feel it more intensely in old age when physical limitations make us more dependent on others. "Old age at some point forces us to accept help from people. It can be hard on the ego, perhaps, because it means acknowledging that we are not in control of the world. But it also gives something valuable to the people who help us."[11]

In 2016, I (Wilkie) learned the value of vulnerability when the chemotherapy to treat my lymphoma flattened me with such fatigue that I had to depend on Noreen just to get through the day. This dependence became a blessing because it opened me up to receiving love in a way that was not possible when I was fit and self-sufficient. While expressions of love and support flooded in from family and friends, Noreen's caring love gave focus to all this inflow of affection. In my journal on July 2, I described my experience: "On our walk this morning, I was struggling to explain to Noreen how this whole experience of cancer and being cared for by her has awakened in me a deeper sense of what a precious gift she is in my life. It is not so much that her loving support surprises me. I've always felt confident in her affection and care. But in these past months, I've been feeling more intensely my love for her." Somewhat frustrated by being unable to share clearly what I was feeling, I stumbled on the "right" words in an unlikely source. I had been reading a book about Zen monastics in Northern California who confronted a wildfire that threatened their beloved Zen center. In the book's afterword, almost as an aside, the author shared a feeling that caught her by surprise when she recalled being with her husband during his bout with cancer.

> Fire will come, welcome or not. Illness comes and with it, fear, pain, loss. Turning away, I realized when my strong, athletic husband suddenly became a cancer patient, is not a workable option. When I look back on John's diagnosis what I feel surprises me. *It is something like longing—for the high relief of that time, for so much love drawn into focus* [emphasis added]. The disease seems to be controlled for now. Some days, I don't think of myeloma at all. I'm lulled into a sense of false permanence, of having something that is mine to keep. Until someone sickens or dies and life reminds me, repeats the hard lesson: *Nothing is for keeps.*[12]

Similarly for me, my chemo-induced vulnerability was a graceful time of high relief when "so much love was drawn into focus."

# SPIRITUAL EXERCISES AND PERSONAL REFLECTIONS

## A. A Prayer for Serenity

Dear God,
Give me the serenity to accept what I cannot change,
The courage to change what I can,
And the wisdom to know the difference.

- When you consider your physical condition, what do you need to accept with serenity?
- When you consider your physical condition, what are changes you can make to benefit your well-being?

## B. The Surrender[13]

Begin by seeking silence.

For this, come home to yourself.
Come to the present.
Ask yourself: Where am I right now?
What am I doing?
What am I thinking?
What am I sensing in my body?
What is the quality of my breathing?

Silence cannot be induced or sought directly.
Just seek awareness—and silence will appear.

If you now wish to communicate with God
within this silence
imagine that you surrender, let go,

# AGING WITH WISDOM AND GRACE

each time you breathe out
—that each exhalation
is your way of saying yes to God.
Yes to what you are today
—to the kind of person God has made you,
the kind of person you have become.
Yes to the whole of your past.
Yes to what lies in store for you in the future.

Let go each time you breathe out
with the awareness that all will be well.
Let all anxieties cease,
and let peace take over
for in his hands, in his will
is our peace.

## Chapter 4

# FROM LOSS TO HOPE

What's lost is nothing to what's found, and all the death that ever was set next to life, would scarcely fill a cup.

—Frederick Buechner

While life entails a continuous series of losses, they seem to cascade in late life. No matter how hard we try, we cannot avoid painful losses. "It is not death that the very old tell me they fear," observes Dr. Atul Gawande in his study of the elderly, "it is what happens short of death—losing their hearing, their memory, their best friend, their way of life."[1]

Passionate investment in life makes us vulnerable to loss. When we think of loss, we naturally think of the death of people we love. We fear, for example, the wrenching grief of being widowed and bereft of the love and companionship that we have grown to depend on. Loss, however, is far more encompassing. Judith Viorst, in her best-selling book on loss, points out that, as we age "we must confront, in the dreams we dream, as well as in our intimate relationships, all that we never will have and never will be....We give up some of our deepest attachments to others."[2] Our losses include "the loss of our own younger self, the self that thought it always would be unwrinkled and invulnerable and immortal."[3] That our journey through life is punctuated by loss is an unavoidable fact.

# Moving through Loss

Given the inevitability of so many losses, we might wonder if it is possible to be content and happy in old age. The view of both social science and Christian faith is yes. In their studies of aging, gerontologists find that a component of elder wisdom is the ability to accept that life does not have to be all good to be good. We can be happy even amid ongoing problems and struggles. Elder wisdom knows that a trouble-free life is illusory and that waiting for all our troubles to go away in order to feel happy is unrealistic. Karl Pillemer of Cornell University distinguishes between "happy in spite of" and "happy if only." The former is "a benefit of old age, the latter a vexation of youth."[4] "Happiness in spite of" entails a choice to be happy even when circumstances of life are less than perfect. Those who are wise experience contentment in life through the acceptance, not the absence of, pain and loss. They don't allow frustrations or anxiety to prevent them from saying they are happy. Consciously or unconsciously, they make the choice to be happy even when there are reasons to feel otherwise.[5]

Christian faith also affirms that life can be happy even amid inevitable loss. The death and resurrection of Jesus, what is referred to as the paschal mystery, is key to the Christian understanding of reality. While theologians may debate what the bodily resurrection of Jesus entailed, they all agree that the early Christians experienced Jesus as a living presence after his death on the cross. "Jesus is alive!"—is, in a nutshell, the contagious good news proclaimed by his early followers. By raising Jesus from the dead, Divine Mystery revealed itself as One who always brings new life from death. Christians are called to view everything in life from the perspective of the paschal mystery, which assures us that wherever we experience loss, diminishment, or death, God will be there to bring forth new life—in some form or another. This is the basis of Christian hope.

The yearly celebration of Easter recalls the central Christian message that the death/resurrection pattern of Jesus's life is also the pattern of our lives. We believe that God will do for us what God did for Jesus—bring new life from death, not only from physical death at the end of life, but also from all our deathlike losses throughout life. This aspect of Christian faith is captured in a poignant prayer:

> My God,
> I can never prepare myself for loss,
> it is always wrenching,
> disorienting.
> But help me to trust
> that each loss can teach me
> not to cling so tightly;
> to let go, to fall
> into the unknown
> where you lie waiting
> to meet me.
> All will be lost:
> my loved ones,
> my body, my life.
> But you have promised
> that all that is lost
> will be found again in you.
> Help me find the riches
> hidden in my loss,
> the rock-certainty of your love
> in the swirling rapids of change.
> Help me to lose
> that I may gain.

# AGING WITH WISDOM AND GRACE

May all my losses
lead me back to you.[6]

The paschal mystery—God's gift of new life through loss—
expresses Christianity's secret to living with hope. Throughout life,
we experience "deaths" of many kinds—the death of our youth, the
death of our dreams, the death of romantic illusions, the death of
inadequate images of God and self. At each point of dying, we can
only undergo rebirth by letting go of the past and being open to something new. Clinging to youth, for example, does not slow down the
aging process but rather prevents us from growing in self-acceptance.
Holding on to something that is meant to be released can only lead
to misery. Christian faith encourages us to let go and to trust that the
God who once gave life will now renew it in an even deeper way.

A framework that puts loss in a hopeful context is provided by
Old Testament scholar Walter Brueggemann, who describes spirituality as our walk with God through the following recurrent pattern:

- being securely oriented
- being painfully disoriented
- being surprisingly reoriented

This pattern repeats itself in all areas of our lives where we
encounter the divine: in relation to the self, others, and the
world. Brueggemann's map of the rhythms of human life likely
corresponds to our own experience. If we reflect on our life history,
we will recognize the phases he describes. Periods of being securely
oriented are marked by a sense of well-being and security: good
health, rewarding work, loving family, close friends, and money
in the bank. Yet we know too well that these moments of security
can be quickly shattered. All it takes is the quiet invasion of a
microscopic virus to compromise our immune system and lay us
low or a disturbing telephone call to inform us that a loved one has
been diagnosed with terminal cancer. Earthquakes and wildfires,

as well as other unpredictable forces of nature, remind us that the phase of painful disorientation can make a sudden entrance, dramatically changing the landscape of our lives.

The phase of being painfully disoriented represents a time when loss has occurred and we struggle with the chaos resulting from the breakdown of something familiar, like a relationship. Here we are challenged to let go of our attachment to that which is lost and to discern the newness that we are called to own. The phase of surprising reorientation happens when during our struggle with painful loss and inner turmoil we feel an energy within our heart to embrace something new. Because this energy to move forward in life seems to have no human origin, we know that God's power of re-creation has dawned again in our life.[7] Surprising reorientation points to the life-giving presence of the God who raised Jesus from the dead.

Because we have survived stormy seasons, we know from experience that life is fluid—we change, people and circumstances change. Losses—such as death, divorce, illness, or disability—fashion a free space where new perceptions (like faith, hope, and love) may find hospitality. Disruptive life circumstances "can dismantle the complacent sensibilities we have thus far cultivated and send us seeking. We are stripped bare in the breech. Unmasked in the unfamiliar disequilibrium. In our nakedness we are somehow more vulnerable to the divine touch."[8] Then, in mysterious and graceful ways, our struggles abate. Perhaps after months or years of grieving the loss of a loved one, the tears finally dry up and a desire to reengage with life emerges. Grandchildren are born and their needs rekindle our capacity to nurture life. And our lives are surprisingly resituated as we move beyond our grief.

# The Ongoing Rebirth of Trust

Jesus taught that the secret to maintaining hope amid loss lies in ongoing rebirth. This was his message to Nicodemus, a senior

Pharisee who came to him in search of wisdom (see John 3:1–10). Nicodemus found Jesus's teaching puzzling. And with Nicodemus, we too ask, "How can grown people be reborn? Can they go back into their mothers' wombs and be born again?" For Jesus, the heart of spiritual transformation entails dying to that part of us that resists trusting God and the rebirth of that part of us that knows of God's reliability and love. We undergo rebirth again and again each time we fall back on ourselves and act as if God is disinterested and far from us. "Dying describes a mode of existence we agree to once we enter the holy space of being a follower of Jesus—surrendering control, dying, all the time."[9] The first three steps of twelve-step spirituality embody well the wisdom of Jesus regarding spiritual transformation. Whenever we are blinded by the illusion of control, the recovery of sanity lies in once again turning our will and our lives over to God's care. Admitting our powerlessness opens the way to a trustful surrender to God. Jesus insisted that we have to be born *anothen*. The Greek word is significant because it has a double meaning: "again and again" and "from above." Letting go and letting God is a continual challenge, not something accomplished once and for all. Over the course of our lifetime, our ongoing efforts to hand over to God what we cannot control hone our ability to say "Amen" in accepting illness, loss, and finally death. In facing this challenge, we can take comfort in Jesus's reassurance to Nicodemus that our efforts are always aided by God's Spirit "from above."

# Grieving Our Losses

Faith tells us that we survive the tailspins of heartache and loss by letting go and moving on. To live vibrantly requires refusing to be immobilized by the inevitable losses of life and continuing to walk ahead with trust in the life-giving power of God—available to us at every point on our journey. The losses we endure must be grieved so that we can move on in a healthy way. Grieving, the complex psychological process of acknowledging and accepting loss, is important because it releases energy that is tied to whatever we have lost—whether a relationship, a much-anticipated opportunity, or desired life goal. This "freed up" energy can then be directed to new, life-giving possibilities. Ungrieved losses bind us to the past. "Rightly did Ovid claim that 'suppressed grief suffocates' creativity or openness to newness," observes Gerald Arbuckle, who argues for the importance of cultural and institutional grieving as a prelude for transforming moribund structures in the church and society.[10]

Elizabeth Kübler-Ross's stages of dying shed light on the complex emotional process of letting go. Significant loss can set off a painful swirl of feelings—such as anger, sadness, disbelief, resistance, and hopelessness. Dealing with these feelings is an important part of the grieving process. While there is a natural tendency in us to turn away from pain, it is important, writes Ram Dass, to "open to it as fully as possible and allow our hearts to break. We must take enough time to remember our losses—be they friends or loved ones passed away, the death of long-held hopes or dreams, the loss of homes, careers, or countries, or health we may never get back again. Rather than close ourselves to grief, it helps to realize that we only grieve for what we love."[11] Healthy grieving allows us to remember the importance of our loss and to experience a newfound peace in place of lingering pain.

Because grieving is a deeply personal process, we must honor individual differences in the ways we and others deal with loss. Some prefer to grieve in private; others find a support group helpful. For some of us, grieving a major loss may take months; for others, it may take years. Mourning has no set timetable. When we expect a person "to get over it" after a certain time has passed, we are not respecting their natural rhythm and individuality. When grieving, there are no rules of right and wrong. Allowing ourselves to truly feel and process our feelings in our own way, taking all the time we need, is a way to accept our pain without adding to our suffering.

# AGING WITH WISDOM AND GRACE

A true story of a sixty-eight-year-old retired hotel worker illustrates how healthy grieving can take many forms, sometimes quite outside of the ordinary! As reported in the *Los Angeles Times*, a woman spent $4,100 in cab fare on a whimsical ride from her home in Pasadena, California, to Victoria, Canada, to get out of a slump. Feeling down because of the death of a friend, the woman called a Los Angeles Yellow Cab for a lift. "I love riding along the ocean—I guess I could have gone to Santa Monica. But I said, 'Let's go to Santa Barbara.' When we got there I didn't want to stop. I said, 'Let's keep going north.'"[12] Having never been north of San Francisco, the grieving woman directed the cab driver to make what turned out to be a nine-day, 3,128-mile trip.

The cab, with "City of Los Angeles Taxi" decals on its yellow doors, attracted a lot of attention as it wound its way up the coast into the Pacific Northwest and eventually rolled onto a ferry at Port Angeles, Washington, for the trip to Victoria, Canada. She reported, "Kids would hang out of vans when they drove past and yell, 'Hey, baby! Go for it!' People stopped us to ask if we were lost or if the cab was a movie prop." Later, when interviewed on television, the woman, dubbed "the little old lady from Pasadena" on the front page of a Seattle newspaper admitted, "It's the most impulsive thing I've ever done." Yet for her, the taxi trip did the trick. It snapped her out of her blue mood. "I never laughed so much in my life as I did the last nine days," she confessed when she returned home. "I'll never be depressed again." Sometimes it takes doing something altogether different to grieve a significant loss and to keep from getting stuck in sadness.

There are several important dimensions to grieving, no matter our personal psychological makeup and circumstances. The process of grieving is "heart work" with no logical order. Our sadness may come in waves, surprising us at times, when we thought we had finished grieving. We know intuitively when our grief recedes, because something in us urges us to move on.

*Naming and Owning the Loss*: Acknowledging and naming the

loss, for example, "My divorce not only ended a relationship, but it also was the death of a dream and made me feel like a failure." Or, "The death of my child feels so wrong. It feels unnatural to be burying her, when she should have outlived me." Loss is a complex experience. As we get older, we may feel the burden of accumulated loss, the pool of grief that has been collected over a lifetime of sorrowful separations from loved ones—parents, siblings, and friends. A current disappointment or heartache may trigger old grief and cause a depth of sadness that seems disproportionate to what we have just lost. Instead of minimizing our feelings, confusing as they might be, it is important to pay attention to anything that surfaces as we grieve.

*Honoring Our Pain with Self-Compassion:* It is also important to honor our feelings and allow ourselves to be bereft and disoriented. Self-compassion means that we do not judge or criticize ourselves for feeling the way we do. An inner voice might, for example, interrupt the flow of our feelings by telling us that we don't have a right to feel a certain way or that we wouldn't be feeling the way we do if we were more mature, spiritual, or unselfish. We don't need to apologize for our feelings or for our tears. The suppression of feelings affects us, consciously or unconsciously, in unhealthy ways. Feeling the pressure to "resume life as normal" can tempt us to prematurely end the process, leaving certain feelings unacknowledged. When the grief process is stalled, we lack the emotional closure that allows us to move on with our life.

*Sharing Our Pain:* It is said that happiness shared is doubled and sorrow shared is halved. Grief heals when it is received by someone who cares and can witness tenderly to our sorrow. By sharing our feelings with God and others, we allow ourselves to be comforted in our grief. Significant loss can evoke a wide range of emotions. We may feel bereft, angry, hurt, abandoned, lonely, betrayed, guilty, lost, hopeless, or helpless. The intensity of these feelings can surprise and frighten us. It is important to share honestly all we are feeling with someone we trust without fear of being judged or criticized by them.

*Embodying Our Readiness to Move On*: When we have sufficiently mourned our loss (though tears and sadness may still come unbidden and an old sorrow may ambush us at any time), we will move on. It can be helpful to ritualize through some symbolic action our letting go of what has been lost and our desire to move on. The ritual action can be done alone or with others. The Jewish tradition of sitting *shiva* and the traditional Irish wake are ritual outlets for grieving. On a personal level, a symbolic act might take the form of giving away the clothes of a deceased loved one or joining a social group at church to meet new friends.

*Reengaging with Our Life*: Reengaging with life after a time of mourning is a natural, rather than a forced, movement forward. It is characterized by hope that satisfaction and joy can once again be ours.

# SPIRITUAL EXERCISES AND PERSONAL REFLECTIONS

## A. Letting God Console Us in Our Grief

To enter into this kind of intimate prayer in which we allow ourselves to be transparent before God, we must trust God enough to expose our vulnerability and pain. Jesus is the compassion of God made flesh, so that through his humanity we can experience divine compassion in our many losses in life. With Mary and Martha, we need to have confidence that God will embrace and hold us in our grief.

1. Slowly read the passage of Jesus at the tomb of his friend Lazarus (John 11:1–53).
2. In your mind's eye, imagine Jesus as he encounters those who are grieving over Lazarus's death. "When Jesus saw her [Mary] weeping, and the Jews who came with her also weeping, he was greatly disturbed in spirit and deeply moved" (John 11:33).
3. Imagine Jesus's sadness at the death of his friend. "Jesus began to weep. So the Jews said, "See how he loved him!" (John 11:35–36).
4. Name and reflect on the loss you are experiencing at this time in your life. Let whatever you are feeling surface.
5. Share these feelings with the Jesus who was so moved by Mary and Martha's loss that he wept for them. Let the feelings that you are having be transparent to Jesus, who shares your sorrow, just as he shared the sadness of Lazarus's sisters.
6. As you share your feelings with Jesus, see his tender response to your pain and listen to any words of consolation he might say to you.

# B. Praying Our Goodbyes to All That We Have to Leave Behind

1. Write a letter to God about the goodbyes that are presently in your life...your sense of loss, expectations, fears, and hopes. What do you desire from God in this time for yourself and others?

2. Write a letter from God to you in response. What do you think God might be saying to you in this time and situation? Do any scriptures come to your mind?

3. Looking at what you have written about, what responses, feelings, and prayers are stirred in you? What have you learned? Relearned? Been surprised by?

# Chapter 5

# CONSIDERING OUR "EXPIRATION DATE"

I often feel that death is not the enemy of life, but its friend, for it is the knowledge that our years are limited which makes them so precious.

—Rabbi Joshua L. Liebman[1]

That we will expire is certain; when and how are shrouded in mystery. We are not surprised when batteries in our flashlight die and need to be replaced. They have a built-in capacity and sooner or later lose their charge. Like batteries, we too have a "limited charge." The stark biological reality is that eventually our bodies will fail in some way: blocked circulation, the inadequate flow of oxygen to tissues, the flickering out of brain functions, the failure of organs and other vital centers. Given this fact, why do we see death as a pitched battle that must be won?

A prevalent view of death in our society is that death is the enemy, "a grim adversary to be overcome, whether with the dramatic armament of high-tech biomedicine or by a conscious acquiescence to its power," notes Dr. Sherwin Nuland in his candid portrayal of the experience of dying.[2] His book *How We Die* illustrates with insightful vignettes how the human body is not built to last forever. Death is "simply an event in the sequence of nature's ongoing rhythm. Not death but disease is the real enemy, disease the malign force that requires confrontation. Death is the surcease that comes when the exhausting battle has been lost....Every triumph over some major pathology, no matter how ringing the victory, is only a reprieve from the inevitable end."[3] Nuland's sensitive reflections about life's final chapter encourage us to accept our dying with less fear and desperation.

Spiritual director Susan Jorgensen uses the image of death as a bookend to convey her understanding that death is a natural part of life, with the first bookend being birth and the second, death. In her work *The Second Bookend: Completing a Life*, she shares her personal experience of dying with honesty and soulfulness. Faced with a diagnosis of terminal cancer in her early sixties, she devoted her last year to writing about this final leg of her journey. Her heartfelt message, a parting gift to her readers, can be simply stated: to "view death as completely separate from life" places us "literally at a dead end....But to place death intimately *inside* life opens us up to limitless possibilities and an even deeper connection with life."[4] Establishing a conscious relationship with death "will help all of us expand and open our hearts to the completion and beauty that is as real and as present in our passing as are the tragedy and sorrow." The foreword is appropriately laudatory in tone: "Susan's capacity to hold both grief and love while dying indicated a level of spiritual maturity, the capacity to accept *what is* with equanimity," writes her friend Rachel Harris, PhD. "Yes, she cried. Yes, she resisted. Yes, she said, 'This is harder than I thought.' And yet she always returned to her spiritual process of attuning to the mystery, and there she found comfort and support....*The Second Bookend* is a rare glimpse into the process of completing a life in preparation for death."[5]

Jorgensen's theme resonates with the "conscious dying" movement and the message of such thinkers as the late Stephen Levine, who worked with the dying for over twenty years. In his work, he noticed how often death takes people unaware, even those who had months or even years of illness to prepare themselves. As they approach the precipice and look back on their lives, they are often overwhelmed by a sense of failure and regret. For so long, they tolerated unsatisfying work, unfinished business in important relationships, and a compromised lifestyle, rationalizing that they would make changes "later." But "later" came sooner than expected, leaving them facing death feeling frustrated and incomplete. As the saying goes, "It's always too soon, until it's too late." This recognition inspired his book *A Year to Live*, which challenges the reader "to live this year as if it were your last." He proposes that we take a year "to live as consciously as possible, a year to finish business, to catch up with our lives, to investigate and deal with our fear of death, to cultivate our true heart and find our essential wisdom and joy. A year to live as if that is all that remains."[6]

# Our Own Deepest Desires

What would you do if you had only one year to live? What do you want to be caught dead doing? Questions such as these are meant to promote living with as much satisfaction as possible. They aim to heighten our awareness of how we truly want to live our life. On our deathbed, what would we be able to ratify with satisfaction about our present way of living and what would we regret? A story is told of St. Alphonsus Rodriquez, a Jesuit lay brother who served as the porter at a Jesuit residence in Majorca for forty-six years until his death in 1617. Daily, he cheerfully greeted guests at the door. One day, he was asked what he would change in his life if he were told he had only twenty-four hours to live. He answered without hesitation, "I would change nothing. I'd just keep living as I do." In June 2018, shortly before his death at age sixty-eight, the well-known Fox News commentator Charles Krauthammer expressed his gratitude for a full life. In a letter published in the

*Washington Post*, he announced that his cancer had returned and that he had only a few weeks to live. "I leave this life with no regrets," Krauthammer shared. "It was a wonderful life—full and complete with the great loves and great endeavors that make it worth living. I am sad to leave, but I leave with the knowledge that I lived the life that I intended." He thanked his colleagues and Fox News viewers, saying that he was "grateful to have played a small role in the conversations that have helped guide this extraordinary nation's destiny."[7] Living a life that we can affirm with contentment when we are dying truly makes for a happy ending. In the end, contentment flows from knowing that we have embraced the gift of life with passion and amazement, having taken every opportunity offered, marveling at the world around us—and not, in the words of Mary Oliver, "simply having visited this world."[8]

Viewing our death as the natural culmination of life keeps us from seeing death as something that robs or cheats us. Dying is a natural condition of our existence. If we can accept the known and unknown conditions that accompany life, we are able to appreciate with profound gratitude the precious gift that life is. Death is not an abrupt breaking off from life, but a new stage of the process in our body's gradual yet inexorable journey back to dust from which we were made by a loving Creator. This return to God is hopeful, not something to be feared. Jesus reassures us that "unless a grain of wheat falls into the earth and dies, it remains just a single grain; but if it dies, it bears much fruit (John 12:24). These words sum up the core of the wisdom and promise of Jesus: God will always bring new life where we experience death and diminishment.

A balanced and peaceful approach to life challenges us to keep two seemingly opposite attitudes in creative tension. On the one hand, to treasure our life as a precious possession and, on the other hand, to hold on to it lightly, as a delicate gift that is sustained at every moment by the breath of God. T. S. Eliot gives poetic expression to the need to cherish life without desperately clinging to it. His poem "Ash Wednesday" affirms the beauty and preciousness of the gift of time and place, even in their fleeting nature. At the same time, it encourages us not to be anxious about holding on to what we enjoy, but "to sit still."

> Because I know that time is always time
> And place is always and only place
> And what is actual is actual only for one time
> And only for one place
> I rejoice that things are as they are....
>
> Teach us to care and not to care
> Teach us to sit still.
>
> Pray for us sinners now and at the hour of our death
> Pray for us now and at the hour of our death.[9]

In sharing what he would do were he diagnosed with terminal cancer, Michael Lerner, a MacArthur "genius award" recipient, illustrates a stance that combines caring deeply for the gift of life and facing death with serenity. "I would strive for life and recovery, with every possible tool and resource I could find. But I would also work to face death in a way that deepened my growth and led to some resolution."[10] His words echo the wisdom of the conscious dying movement: "I would do everything that I could do that I didn't want to leave undone....I would try to live my life in my own way. I would try to accept the pain and sorrow inherent in my situation, but I would look searchingly for the beauty, wisdom, and the joy."[11]

# Jesus's Prayer Shows Us the Way

Jesus's prayer of agony in the Garden of Gethsemane reveals that Jesus knew how "to care and not to care." Feeling "distressed and agitated," Jesus said to Peter, James, and John who accompanied him, "'I am deeply grieved, even to death; remain here, and keep awake.' And going a little farther, he threw himself on the ground and prayed that, if it were possible, the hour might pass from him. He said, 'Abba, Father, for you all things are possible; remove this cup from me; yet, not what I want, but what you want'" (Mark 14:33–36). It is significant to note that, in the Greek, the verbs "*threw* himself on the ground and *prayed*" are in the imperfect tense. Grammatically, the imperfect tense signifies an ongoing action in the past. In other words, the verse communicates a repeated action and a prayer that lasted awhile, not just a moment. Literally, Jesus *kept throwing* himself on the ground and *kept praying*. It exposes the anguish of a Jesus who, as a young man, was facing an untimely death and an abrupt end to his ministry. It portrays Jesus as someone with a robust appreciation of life and a passionate desire to continue his work. Clearly, he cared deeply and did not want to walk gently into the night. Yet, in Jesus, there is noticeably no "rage against the dying of the light."

Instead, Jesus ends his prayerful plea to be spared with a trusting surrender to God: "Yet, not what I want, but what you want." The two parts of his prayer—pleading for a pass and accepting his fate—are held together by the Aramaic term *Abba*, his name for God. *Abba* is a term that connotes intimacy and closeness; to Jesus, God was not a distant and mighty deity who had to be obeyed, but a loving "papa, daddy." That the Aramaic term was kept in the Greek text is significant because it indicates that Jesus's acceptance of his death was not a coerced acquiescence to a demanding God, but a trusting surrender to a loving God, whose promise of new life from death could be relied upon. Confident in the enduring love of God, Jesus was able to care and not to care.

# Thriving in God's Hands

Embodying an ardent zeal for his work, as well as a peaceful acceptance of his diminished capacity, the late Jesuit leader Pedro

Arrupe modeled how "to care and not to care." In him, we can detect the pattern of Jesus, who pursued his ministry with resolute determination, yet was willing to let go in trust. Arrupe was superior general of the Jesuits for eighteen years. After many years as a missionary in Japan, he was called to Rome to lead the worldwide Society of Jesus during a tumultuous time of conflict and change both in the world and the Church. The stressful nature of his position contributed to his failing health and ultimately to a debilitating stroke. Father Arrupe's farewell message, addressed to the governing body of the Jesuits on September 3, 1983, revealed the exuberant spirit that kept him vibrant, even in the midst of severe physical decline. Rendered unable to speak by his stroke, this multilingual leader had to rely on someone to read his speech. Nevertheless, even when conveyed through the voice of another, his message evoked tearful gratitude in his brother Jesuits. With characteristic warmth, Arrupe shared the meaning of this final chapter of his life:

> How I wish I were in a better condition for this meeting with you! As you see, I cannot even address you directly.
>
> More than ever, I now find myself in the hands of God. This is what I have wanted all my life, from my youth. And this is still the one thing I want. But now there is a difference: the initiative is entirely with God. It is indeed a profound spiritual experience to know and to feel myself so totally in his hands.

In Holy Week of 2004, while consulting for the Lilly Endowment in Indianapolis, Bill Spohn, the late moral theologian and our good friend, suffered seizures that scrambled his speech and landed him in the hospital. This sudden intrusion of illness led to a diagnosis of brain cancer and then death at age sixty-one, after a relatively brief period of treatment. During this time, his emails to friends were a final gift from this brilliant and faith-filled man, whose faith led him to distinguish between resignation and surrender. Resignation feels like "this is just the way it is, so 'tough it out,'" he wrote, while surrender "is not giving up, but saying 'Into Your hands I commend my spirit, O Lord.'"[12] Surrender was not always easy, he admitted. "There are times when there isn't much energy for surrender and then it seems more like resignation. But fortunately, those times are rare." In the end, Bill summed up beautifully what enabled him to surrender in trust. While he realized that some people could chalk up his attitude of faith to "deep reservoirs of denial," he adamantly differed.

> Our thoughts are somewhat different. Who knows, God's ways may be surprisingly better than the scripture of Kubler-Ross and all the other gurus of grief. Yes, there are undeniable losses, but they don't compare with the advent of God's approach. In the original context of Isaiah, "God's ways" refers to a goodness that takes our breath away. Most of this is not mystical or abstract. It comes in very concrete ways, primarily through other people.[13]

Having been a Jesuit for thirty-two years, Bill embodied the spirituality of Ignatius of Loyola in his peaceful acceptance of death, at the relatively young age of sixty-one, when he was at the height of his career as a moral theologian. In his last email, he shared the sad news that the doctors had confirmed that the tumor had once again grown back, or as one of his doctors put it, "Clearly, you failed the trial drug." His wife, Marty, describes the immediate events that led to Bill's final yes to God's call to return to the loving source from which he came.[14]

> We had the scan Thursday a week ago, then met with the surgeon the following day at 9 a.m. He would give us the first read on the scan. We had to drive into the city during rush hour, so we read the lessons for the day before tackling the traffic. The text was John 21:15–19, the

passage where Jesus questions Peter again and again: "Do you love me?" After Peter's repeated professions of love, Jesus says to him, "When you were younger, you used to fasten your own belt and go wherever you wished. But when you grow old, you will stretch out your hands, and someone else will fasten a belt around you and take you where you do not wish to go. Follow me." It was hard driving across the Bay Bridge with that text in our hearts. But we got to the city early and went up to the University of San Francisco campus. Always we were drawn to the side chapel and to St. Ignatius's *Suscipe* on the wall. The first part of that prayer is a pretty accurate description of brain cancer, and that terrified us both, but the second part offered the consolation we craved.

Take, Lord, receive all my liberty,
my memory, my understanding,
and my entire will,
All that I am and call my own.

You have given it all to me.
To you, Lord, I return it.
Everything is yours, do with it what you will.

Give me only your love and your grace.
That is enough for me.

In the end, this prayerful surrender to a beckoning God reflected the faith that shaped Bill's life as a Christian. Because of that *Suscipe* prayer, he wrote, "We were ready when the surgeon told us that the tumor had grown back. And we were ready when he said the chemo had not been working. We are living inside that prayer. All things considered, it is not a bad place to be. You are part of this journey more than you know.

The love that we experience through you not only helps us along the way, but is already the beginning of the abundant life to come."

Anyone who knew Bill Spohn knew how much he loved life. Yet he was willing to hold life lightly and to place it trustfully into God's care. This is what the Jesuit poet Gerard Manley Hopkins invites us to do whatever the circumstances of our lives. He encourages us to hand over our life—with all its worries and struggles, delights and beauty—to God's keeping and to give it now:

> …deliver it, early now, long before death
> Give beauty back, beauty, beauty, beauty, back to God,
>     beauty's self and beauty's giver.
> See; not a hair is, not an eyelash, not the least lash lost;
>     every hair
> Is, hair of the head, numbered….
>
> O then, weary then whý should we tread? O why are
>     we so haggard at the heart, so care-coiled,
>     care-killed, so fagged, so fashed, so cogged, so
>     cumbered,
> When the thing we freely fórfeit is kept with fonder a
>     care
> Fonder a care kept than we could have kept it….
>
> (excerpted from "The Golden Echo")[15]

# Dying as a Personal Experience

A late-night comic quips, "The findings of a recent, large-scale study conclude that 'ten out of ten people will die of something!'"

Yes, death is universal, but it is also deeply personal. Our uniqueness as individuals extends even to the way we die. In describing the various ways in which death approaches, Dr. Nuland notes, "Everyone of death's diverse appearances is as distinctive as that singular face we each show the world during the days of life. Every man will yield up the ghost in a manner that the heavens have never known before; every woman will go her final way in her own way."[16] No wonder we find ourselves at times thinking about when, how, and where we will make our exit from the stage of life. Such personal musings peak our curiosity as we comb daily through the obituary page: How old was the deceased? What was the cause and circumstances of their death? At times, our wondering is tinged with anxiety about how and when we will face our own death.

Perhaps that is why we find comfort and courage in the last testaments of Pedro Arrupe, Susan Jorgenson, and Bill Spohn, who each shared how they viewed their dying and the personal meaning of their final passage. Arrupe described his debilitating stroke as yet another experience of being placed in God's hands. Jorgenson framed her dying as the second bookend, a natural ending to a life for which she was deeply grateful. And Spohn experienced his dying as surrendering to a "goodness that takes our breath away." In these final testimonies, they showed us how to approach death and dying in a healthy and personally meaningful way, each writing the final chapter to their own life story. Palliative care workers talk about "the dying role." As people approach the end of their life, they want to share memories, pass on wisdom, make peace with God, settle relationships, and ensure that those left behind will be okay. The dying "want to end their stories on their own terms. This role is…among life's most important, for both the dying and those left behind."[17]

Ira Byock, one of the nation's foremost authorities on palliative care and an expert on dying well, has witnessed in people who are dying "a sense of wellness and peace that can only be called blissful." "Despite the arduous nature of the experience," he writes, "when people are relatively comfortable and know that they are not going to be abandoned, they frequently find ways to strengthen bonds with people they love and to create moments of profound meaning in their final passage."[18] He suggests four simple phrases that have the power to mend relationships and to bring emotional healing when approaching our end: "Thank you," "Please forgive me," "I forgive you," and "I love you." These four phrases enable people to fulfill their "dying role" and to experience a sense of wholeness in the face of death. The process of dying provides us with the precious opportunity to lighten up a burdened spirit by letting go of grudges and to restore valued relationships that have been painfully ruptured. "I have seen many die, surrounded by loved ones," writes Levine, "and their last words were 'I love you.' There were some who could no longer speak, yet with their eyes and soft smile, left behind that same healing. I have been in rooms where those who were dying made it feel like sacred ground."[19]

# Anxiety about *How* We Will Die

After hearing the risen Jesus convey the kind of death he would endure for God's glory, Peter spotted his close friend John and asked Jesus, "What about him, Lord?" Jesus answered, "If I want him to stay behind till I come, what does it matter to you? You are to follow me" (John 21:20–23 NJB). In saying this, Jesus was encouraging Peter to stay focused on his own path and to trust in God's love for him—a love that would extend to the very moment of death. Jesus's message to Peter about God's provident love is something that can also reassure our anxious hearts. We need not worry that God will ever abandon us. A divine gaze regards everything we hold precious and shapes God's individual care for each of us. "Can you not buy two sparrows for a penny? And yet not one falls to the ground without your Father knowing. Why, every hair on your head has been counted. So there is no need to be afraid" (Matt 10:29–31 NJB). Shakespeare echoes this biblical faith: "There's a special providence in the fall of a sparrow. If it be now, 'tis not to come. If it be not to come, it will be now. If it be not now, yet it will come—the readiness is all."[20]

## Considering Our "Expiration Date"

We also find ourselves wondering what we can expect after we die. In this life, the best we get is a "taste of heaven"— "heaven" being that emotionally charged religious symbol of the final fulfillment of our heart's deepest longing. "Earth's crammed with heaven," writes poet Elizabeth Barrett Browning—an elegant reminder that we don't have to wait until we die to experience heaven. In poetic language, she alludes to the theological notion of "inaugurated eschatology"—that the "eternal life" that we hope for at death is "already" here, but not fully, "not yet." We can enjoy experiences of "heaven" in the here and now, as well as look forward to a greater fullness of heavenly joy in the hereafter. Our here-and-now experience of the Spirit—in moments of peace, love, joy, patience, kindness, goodness (Gal 5:22–23)—constitutes a foretaste of what God has in store for us in the hereafter. Through Jesus and the gift of the Spirit, we already experience something of resurrection life, the fullness of which we will experience after death. It is *this experience of the future in the present* that provides us with vibrant hope for what is promised us after death.

We experience "a taste of heaven" in moments of profound love, beauty, joy, and peace in God's presence—times when we feel swept up into another realm. Such religious experiences so enthrall us that we lose track of time and place. Nonetheless, they are momentary and fleeting. If we try to cling to them or try to control them, we lose the moment. Like Peter, James, and John, who accompanied Jesus up the mountain and witnessed the transfiguration, we too can be surprised by experiences that are so saturated by divinity that we feel like "we're in heaven." And like the apostles who wanted to "lock in" their peak experience by building tents, we share the human tendency to cling to such graceful moments only to lose them through our grasping. The promise that sustains hope is this: at death, we will experience something as awesome as these moments of pure joy and delight—but the pivotal difference is that there will be no end. The ecstasy at the end will be endless.

"Heaven" is a state of perpetual happiness; we will feel no lack. Nothing we need for happiness will be missing.

# Hope Grounded in Our Experience

Optimism is holding a belief without any grounding in evidence. It is merely a gratuitous assertion, like the myth of progress that blithely asserts that things will always get better. Hope is not the same as optimism. In contrast, hope is rooted in our experience; the seeds of hope are memories of actual experiences when we have felt God's presence in a way that wraps us securely in a blanket of profound peace and happiness. "We cannot hope in the future without reference to our faith in God who has been active in the past and the present," theologian Dermot Lane states. "Hope and the possibility of eternal life, therefore, is not some kind of idle speculation or personal projection without reference to the experience of God in the present. Instead, hope is a particular interpretation of the promise present or absent in human experiences. As such, hope is a trusting interpretation that the glimpses of life and beauty and glory in the present are not empty but full of promise."[21] Hope sustains trust in God's ultimate graciousness even in the face of life's ambiguous mixture of joy and grief, loss and creativity, suspicion and trust.

We are meant to live with hopeful anticipation of a future good that outstrips our imagination. On this side of the grave, our moments of experiencing God's presence have a paradoxical quality: they simultaneously satisfy a deep hunger in us and whet our appetite for more. Often, at large gatherings when eating utensils are limited, people at table are asked to hang on to their forks after finishing their salad or appetizer, to use with the main dish. Based on this common occurrence and the biblical metaphor of the afterlife as a messianic banquet, a preacher once exhorted his congregation to walk through life hanging on to their forks because "the best is yet to come."

A wedding banquet is a common metaphor for the mystery symbolized by "heaven." The story of Jesus changing over a hundred gallons of water into fine wine at a wedding in the village of Cana amplifies the metaphor with vivid details. John's Gospel features the wedding at Cana as the dramatic opening scene of Jesus's public ministry and uses this inaugural story to say what the story of Jesus is about, what constitutes the good news. To the early readers of John's account, mention of marriage and a wedding carried important significance. As a rich religious metaphor, marriage evoked the covenant relationship between God and Israel and between Christ and his bride, the Church. Moreover, a wedding feast in the hard and meager existence of Jewish peasant life at the time of Jesus was the most festive of celebrations, a momentary release from unremitting hard work and an occasion to enjoy a time of plenty, filled with food, wine, music, and dancing. Given this context, it is easy to see why the opening story of the wedding feast at Cana was a powerful way of conveying the good news: *"the story of Jesus is about a wedding.* And more: it is a wedding at which the wine never runs out. More: it is a wedding at which the best wine is saved for last."[22]

# In the End All Shall Be Well

When facing our death, it is natural to feel the kind of fear that the unknown stirs up in us. The words of Julian of Norwich, a fourteenth-century mystic, reassure us that in the end "all will be well." Hers was a century racked by pain and chaos: the black plague was devastating Europe, causing disaster on an unprecedented scale (not unlike the AIDS epidemic in Africa), severe crop failures threatened the onslaught of a famine at a time when the economic resources of both England and France had been completely drained by the Hundred Years' War. In addition, Europe was convulsing through a complex transition triggered by the demise of feudalism and the emergence of nationalism and the mercantile system (not unlike the upheaval in Russia after the breakup of the Soviet Union and the switch from a centralized to a free market economy).

Surrounded by these chaotic conditions, Julian was able to live with trust and gratitude; her religious experience revealed to her that in the end "all will be well." She was reassured that no matter how fragile life seems, God, like our clothing "wraps and enfolds us for love, embraces us and shelters us, surrounds us for love."[23] This wondrous insight came to her as she contemplated an image of something tiny in her hand, not much bigger than a hazelnut. As she gazed at this small object, she was amazed at its ongoing existence. How is something so tiny and fragile able to survive in a universe so fraught with dangers? Her heart was then illuminated to understand that the tiny object before her, as well as everything else in the universe, is held safely in God's hands.

> It lasts and always will last because God loves it; and thus everything has being through the love of God. In this little thing I saw three properties. The first is that God made it, the second is that God loves it, and the third is that God preserves it.[24]

# SPIRITUAL EXERCISES AND PERSONAL REFLECTIONS

## A. Testament of Your Life[25]

Imagine that you are going to die today. You want to spend some time alone to write down for your family and friends a sort of testament for which the points that follow could serve as chapter titles.

- These Things I Have Loved in Life
- These Experiences I Have Cherished
- These Ideas Have Brought Me Liberation
- These Convictions I Have Lived By
- These Things I Have Lived For
- These Risks I Have Taken
- These Sufferings Have Seasoned Me
- These Influences Have Shaped My Life (Persons, Occupations, Books, Events)
- These Scripture Texts Have Lit My Path
- These Are My Life's Accomplishments
- These Persons Are Enshrined in My Heart
- These Are My Unfulfilled Desires

## B. A Funeral Fantasy: Bringing Completion to Relationships

Imagine that your body is resting in a coffin. See the faces of your relatives and friends who have come to view your body and to say goodbye. As they approach, look at each of their faces. What do you imagine the person who is standing before you feels? What feelings are stirred up in you as you see him or her?

Is there something you want to say to someone there—either something that you didn't say when you were alive or something you want to say again one final time? Is there something that you wish that someone there would have said to you, but never did?

To whom might you want to say the following:

- "I love you."
- "Thank you."
- "I forgive you."
- "Please forgive me."

# C. Writing Our Own Obituary

The following is an exercise designed to help us clarify what we deeply hope for in a fulfilled life.

[Name], age_____, died yesterday of _____. He/she was a member of _____. He/she is survived by _____. At the time of his/her death, he/she was working on becoming_____. He/she will be mourned by _____ because _____. The world will suffer the loss of his/her contributions in the areas of_____. He/she always wanted to _____, but he/she was never able to. The body will be _____. Flowers may be sent to _____. In lieu of flowers _____.

# Chapter 6

# DEALING WITH REGRETS AND RESENTMENTS

The blessing of regret is clear—it brings us, if we are willing to face it head on, to the point of being present to this new time of life in an entirely new way. It urges us on to continue becoming.

—Joan Chittister, *The Gift of Years*

"Don't stumble over something behind you," warns Seneca the Younger. As we get older, we can find ourselves revisiting the past and dwelling on experiences that were particularly negative and painful. How often have you found yourself transported in time to a memory of an event that you came to deeply regret? It might be something you did. Or something you failed to do. Remorse for actions or choices that had undesirable consequences is one of the most painful emotions that older adults experience. Failed relationships and jobs, living below our potential out of fear or laziness, misplaced priorities, procrastinating until it is too late—recalling any of these can fill us with regret and flood us with thoughts of "what if" or "if only." "If only I had been born at another time, in another place, had been better looking, taller, shorter, smarter, more outgoing. If only I had different parents, worked harder in school, married a different person…."

The danger of getting weighed down by regrets and disappointments is heightened in later life, when we realize that the opportunities we missed or poor choices we made cannot be undone. Whether it be choosing the wrong profession, not spending enough time with our children, deciding to remain single rather than to marry—any of these regrets can haunt us and overshadow our accomplishments. Ram Dass describes his elderly father's obsession with past regrets and the pain it caused him:

> I recall being with my father at a stage of old age when he could not release the bitterness of his past failures. Dad found himself unable to speak of anything else. The mistakes he'd made, the roads he'd not taken, so colored his consciousness that soon the good he'd done in the world, and the many things that he had achieved, were obfuscated by his regrets until he felt that his life had been nothing but a failure. Fortunately, these stormy seas passed, and before he died, Dad came to see his life more clearly.[1]

Regrets can be a source of chronic shame and self-recrimination, especially if we think that the value of our life is measured more by our failures than by the good we have done.

A character in Edgar Widerman's book *Brothers and Keepers* is a stark example of the way that regret can loom so large in a person's life that it "hangs over one's consciousness like a cloud…."

> We have come too far to turn back now. Too far, too long, too much at stake. We got a sniff of the big time and if we

didn't take our shot wouldn't be nobody to blame but ourselves. And that's heavy. You might live another day, you might live another hundred years but long as you live you have to carry that idea round in your head. You had your shot but you didn't take it. You punked out. Now how a person spozed to live with something like that grinning in his face every day? You hear old people crying the blues about how they could have been this or done that if they only had the chance. How you gon pass that by? Better to die than have to look at yourself every day and say, Yeah. I blew it. Yeah, I let it get away.[2]

For some people, the fact that they can't undo or erase the past makes them feel hopeless about the future. As a seventy-two-year-old client put it, "I've made too many mistakes in my life to think that anything is going to change. I am what I am, nothing can change that." Some months later he came to the realization that he was not too old to learn from his mistakes or to make the necessary changes to ensure that his remaining years would be more satisfying and meaningful. None of us reaches our senior years devoid of regrets and disappointments. There comes a time when we realize that some of our dreams have not come true and that no matter how hard we try, we cannot always make life turn out the way we want. We have to accept that bad things have happened to us or to someone we love. Coming to grips with one's human limitations and imperfections is a humbling but important task of aging. Accepting the past, such as it is, and making peace with ourselves free us from obsessing over things we cannot change and open our eyes to see with gratitude all the blessings we have received. Aging with wisdom and grace is only possible when we learn that just because we have made mistakes or our life hasn't turned out the way we thought it would doesn't mean that our future will follow suit. The past doesn't have to determine the future; we have some choice in how our remaining years will play out.

# AGING WITH WISDOM AND GRACE

Decisions that can shape a satisfying future rely on an honest assessment of the present. Regardless of past regrets, what matters is how satisfied we are with how we are living now. If we notice feelings of discontent about any aspect of our present life, we need to figure out what the discontentment is about and what we can do about it.

- Does the discontentment or unrest point to something that we feel is missing in our life? What might that be?
- Does the discontentment point to an unfulfilled desire? Is that desire something we need to let go of at this time in our life or something we need to pursue?
- Is the discontentment or unrest we are feeling a call to accept the limitations of human life or an invitation to imagine creative new possibilities?

Questions like these help us to pinpoint the source of our dis-ease and to see what, if anything, we can do about it. While the contour of much of life's journey is beyond our control, we can, in fact, make choices that help forge a more contented future.

One of the unexpected gifts of aging is the chance to develop aspects of ourselves that were put on hold earlier in life, to resurrect deferred dreams and find new energy and vitality in pursuing them. Older adults often hope to make up for lost time. With children grown, mortgages paid off, and greater financial freedom, this stage of life provides a rich opportunity to focus on our own lives and consider how we want to spend our remaining days—whether that be a matter of years or decades. In her work with the dying, palliative caregiver Bonnie Ware found that people nearing the end of life had several regrets in common. At the top of the list were regrets about not honoring their own dreams or not making changes that would have brought them happiness. "I wish I'd had the courage to live a life true to myself, not the life others expected of me." "I wish that I had let myself be happier." Knowing that the end was near made them look back over their life and acknowledge where they had failed to make choices and changes that would have brought greater satisfaction and meaning.

# Learning from Regrets

Psychiatrist Irwin Yalom believes that regrets serve a meaningful purpose if they help us identify what we still long for. Pointing to the value of regrets, he states, "Properly used, regret is a tool that can help you take actions to prevent its further accumulation." Focusing on past regrets only to sink into sadness is not helpful. However, if we look to the future, we "experience the possibility of either amassing more regret or living relatively free of it." He encourages his aging patients to use their regrets and fear of death to motivate them to do the things they have always wanted to do. "Imagine one year or five years ahead and think of the regrets that will have piled up in that period....How can you live now without building new regrets? What do you have to change in your life?"[3]

In his *Happiness Is a Choice You Make*, John Leland suggests a similar approach to reducing future regrets, based on a strategy used by chess players, whereby one works backward from an endgame and figures out what sequence of moves led to the desired end. Applying this analogy to aging, he suggests that we look ahead to what we want our life to be like at seventy-five, eighty, or eighty-five. We identify what would give meaning and satisfaction to our life then. We ask ourselves, "What pleasures, what rewards, what daily activities and human connections" would make us happy? Then, he suggests working our way backward to see what moves will lead us there. Such clarity helps us to ignore the moves that don't get us where we want to go and to focus on the ones that do. If, for example, you want close supportive relationships, intellectual stimulation, music and art, or to help others, "trace a series of moves leading up to that, all the way back to your present time."[4] Leland's point is that we know what we do not want our old age to be like—we don't want to run out of money, be dependent on others, be left alone and lonely, or have Alzheimer's—but we may not have thought about what we do want. What a creative and proactive way to prepare ourselves for old age!

# Regrets in the Light of Faith

We all can recall times when our words and actions caused pain and suffering. To feel remorse for hurting others is normal and healthy if it moves us to reparation and helps us to avoid repeating our mistakes. Saying "I'm sorry, please forgive me," as hospice physician Ira Byock suggests, is a key to mending ruptured relationships with loved ones. Feeling remorse provides us with opportunities to acknowledge both how we have missed the mark in loving and to make amends for our past shortcomings. Jesuit Jim Harbaugh explains why the Spiritual Exercises and twelve-step spirituality encourage us to look at our past regrets. "During the First Week of the Exercises, Ignatius urges us to consider our past, not in a spirit of 'worry, remorse or morbid reflection' (BB, 86), but in light of chances for service" and the healing of relationships. According to Harbaugh, "A clear view of the past is essential if we are going to behave differently now; we can't regret the clarity that leads to healed relationships." When recovering alcoholics put the lessons they have learned from painful experience into service, the "past is alchemically transmuted into a treasure for other people."[5] What is true for recovering alcoholics is true for all of us. If we allow our suffering to make us more compassionate and caring toward others, we redeem our suffering and give it meaning. There is an important distinction between wallowing in the past and letting the past teach and transform us; one leads to hopelessness, the other to healing.

Christian faith encourages us to accept our regrets and disappointments in life with trust in the loving care of God. In our struggle to accept life on life's terms, we are called to remember that God's ways are not always our ways. Sarah and Elizabeth—two women who gave birth to sons when they were long past childbearing age—are biblical reminders of God's mysterious ways. Trusting in the faithfulness of God is central to the message of Jesus. Thus, we find St. Paul encouraging the community in Rome by reminding them that God works with us in all of our strivings and "all things [will] work together for good" (Rom 8:28), or, as Julian of Norwich puts it, "In the end, all will be well."

Abiding in trust requires that we pay attention to thoughts that spoil our peace of mind and undermine our confidence in God. The "fearful mind," to use an expression of Ram Dass, sets the stage for perpetual distress. "Fearful thoughts arise most commonly due to our tendency to dwell in the past or invent the future," he observes. We worry, "If this bad thing that happened a year ago happens again, what will I do?" As Ram Dass says, "With the future always unknown, the fearful mind is free to create a horror-show of catastrophes, each leading to the next snowball of every-growing panic. There is no end to unchecked fear; as we get older and feel more vulnerable in the world, fear in its myriad forms can become a chronic companion that renders old age a living hell."[6] Dwelling in the past or conjuring up the future can cause us to forget that God is at work in all of it. As a wise spiritual mentor once said, "Don't run ahead of grace." This same wisdom is reflected in the saying in Alcoholics Anonymous, "Just take one day at a time." Serenity comes to us when we learn to live in the present, making peace with the past and trusting that "all shall be well" in the future.

# Dealing with Resentment

It's a common myth that people become bitter and grumpy as they get older. Some do, of course, but it's not the norm. Bitterness and pessimism in late adulthood are the result of unresolved loss and grief suffered earlier in life. Experiences of abuse, betrayal of trust, injustice, and rejection are deeply wounding and leave residual pain that lasts long after the harm was done. Years later, when memories of those events surface, we replay and relive them in ways that affect our emotional, spiritual, and physical well-being. "We attached our feelings to the moment when we were hurt, endowing it with immortality. And we let it assault us every time it comes to mind," observes pastoral theologian Lewis Smedes. "When we hate people who do us wrong, our hate stays alive long after the wrong they did is dead and gone, the way the ashen smell of charred lumber lingers with a burned building long after the fire is out."[7] When painful memories surface, it is an invitation to begin the process of healing, the first step of which is becoming conscious of feelings that have been smoldering for many years. Becoming fully aware, perhaps for the first time, of the hatred and resentment we have been carrying gives us the opportunity to heal the wounds of our past.

When it comes to dealing with past hurts, many of us push them away. It's better, we think, to let sleeping dogs lie. Let the past stay in the past. We might even think there's something wrong with us for being upset over something that happened years ago. But reburying negative feelings doesn't heal the hurt, it just leads to more resentment. As we age, the past catches up with us. Memories of injuries and injustices done to us or to our loved ones can reawaken feelings of anger, hurt, or shame. We have imaginary conversations with people who have harmed us, drudging up grudges we have held on to for years.

Working through the unfinished business of our past has a significant impact on our happiness and well-being. If we do not overcome our resentments by forgiving those who have hurt us, our golden years will be overshadowed by hatred and bitterness.

We all carry the imprint of past experiences in our emotional memories, many of which occurred in our pre-verbal times. As we age, we often feel closer to these early experiences than we have for many years. With more time for reflection, our minds venture back toward the beginning and the traumas that may have occurred there. This gives us an excellent opportunity to clean house, and bring wisdom to bear on these early wounds.[8]

If we hold grudges, if we don't practice forgiveness, we end up stuck with old grievances.

# Grieving and Forgiveness

Forgiveness is a process that must begin with acknowledging that we have been harmed and allowing ourselves to feel the depth of the pain we have suffered. When we resist the grieving process, we sentence ourselves to a lifetime of being a victim; we cling to our grief forever, letting it define us and using it as an excuse for our faults and failures. If we rush the grieving process, forcing ourselves to forgive too soon, we will discover that nothing has changed.

The following is an example of how to begin working through the unfinished business of the past. This three-fold process of grieving paves the way to genuine forgiveness and inner peace:

1. *Fully acknowledge* the harm that was done to you and what you have lost. How has your life been shaped by this experience?
2. *Suffer it.* If you were mistreated, abandoned, abused, or treated unfairly, you must allow yourself to feel all of your feelings and emotions—fear, rage, hatred, sadness, self-pity, misery. These feelings are your grief.
3. *Share it.* Sharing your painful experiences with someone you trust alleviates the shame you feel, especially if you have kept this secret.

It may take months or even years to fully process your grief. Like any therapeutic process, grief work takes as long as it takes and cannot be rushed. You will know when you are ready to forgive.

Social scientists have come to believe that forgiveness is the key to emotional, spiritual, and physical health; and that people who practice forgiveness are happier than those who don't. Yet we live in an eye-for-an-eye world that encourages retaliation and vengeance. Secular society sees forgiveness as neither a social value nor a behavioral norm, but as a sign of weakness that makes us vulnerable to further mistreatment. For Christians, however, forgiveness is a virtue that is grounded in God's forgiveness of us and our call to forgive others as we have been forgiven. Along with love, forgiveness forms the heart of Jesus's teachings. If we find ourselves resistant to forgiving others, it may be that we have some misconception about what forgiveness is. Or we may want to forgive, but either don't know how or wonder if we can ever truly forgive someone who has mistreated us. Although forgiveness, like any other virtue, does not come naturally or easily, most people we have worked with in therapy or spiritual direction find that they are able to practice forgiveness once they learn what genuine forgiveness is and how to do it. Part of learning about forgiveness is understanding that the person who suffers most when we cling to past hurts and resentments is ourselves, because each time we remember what was done to us, we relive it again. Our hate keeps the experience alive long after it is over; and even when the person who hurt us dies, our emotional attachment to the pain lives on. The practice of forgiveness does not mean forgetting or changing the past. It does not excuse the harm that was done to us—what happened was wrong. But it helps us to see that we have the power to end our suffering if we have the courage to release the past.

In the best-selling book *Tuesdays with Morrie*, there is a powerful lesson about forgiveness and the self-inflicted suffering that results from the refusal to forgive. Morrie, who is nearing the end of his life, has never forgiven his close friend for not visiting his wife when she lay dying in the hospital. Although his friend later apologized and asked for forgiveness, admitting that he failed Morrie because of his own fears about illness and death, Morrie would not forgive him. Years later, on his deathbed, Morrie grieves for his friend, now deceased, and is filled with regret for not forgiving him and reconciling. As he begins to cry, he talks about his old friend and comes to the realization that he must forgive himself as well as his friend. "We need to forgive ourselves. For all the things we didn't do. All the things we should have done…forgive yourself, then forgive others." The powerful takeaway from this touching story is that forgiveness puts closure to the unfinished business of the past and frees us from a prison we didn't know we were in.

# Grace and Forgiveness

Often people feel a confusing ambivalence about letting go of the resentment and hatred caused by past hurts. Having lived so long with rage and resentment, adults who, for example, were sexually abused or felt abandoned as children, have mixed feelings about forgiving their offender. One part of them wants to be finally set free from the burdensome weight of bitter pain, but another part may feel attached to those fiery feelings, despite their debilitating effects. Such feelings have, after all, been part of them for so long that they wonder, and perhaps even fear, how they will have to change if those familiar feelings are gone. That God not only desires our healing but nudges us along despite our ambivalence is clearly shown in one woman's experience:

> I woke one morning with a powerful impulse to attend Mass as well as an equally strong desire to go back to sleep. Even more than the extra sleep, I wanted to avoid someone I suspected might attend that liturgy. In the end, I obeyed the inner nudge and went to Mass, where

I immediately encountered the person I had successfully dodged for years.

I cannot put into words what happened that morning. How do you explain the mystery of forgiveness and reconciliation? I can say that finally letting go of the familiar feelings of anger, resentment and bitterness was extraordinarily freeing. When I learned that the person was moving out of state the next morning, I could only marvel at God's timing.[9]

Twelve-step spirituality teaches that self-help alone cannot heal the hatred and resentment caused by past wounds; for this we need God's grace. Often, after years of struggling to do it on our own, a moment of truth may dawn, enabling us to finally accept our powerlessness to heal ourselves. We stop trying to sidestep the painful process of forgiveness by forgetting what happened or forgiving prematurely so as to not feel our pain.

Despair in our own ability to rid ourselves of the pain that chains us to the past becomes a grace that opens us to God's healing power. Such was the experience of Jesuit Greg Boyle as he struggled with "ancient hurts and resentments." During his high school years, he and his father had breakfast together, in silence, each eating his cereal and reading the *LA Times*.

When my dad was finished and got up from the table, he'd need to pass behind me. I'd instinctively scoot in my chair so he had room. But before moving past me, he'd place his empty bowl on the table. Then, standing behind me, he'd massage my neck, his thumbs digging deep. He smelled like Fitch shampoo and Aqua Velva aftershave. The massage didn't last long, but he did it every day, wordlessly.

Thirty years later, I'm on a silent retreat in a monastery in the California redwoods, sitting in the chapel and not having a good morning. I'm rehashing old story lines: ancient hurts and resentments. The soreness in my soul is palpable—enveloping me, actually. I'm in a chair in the last row, off to the side. There are huge windows behind me, the massive redwoods visible in the early morning sunlight.

Suddenly, I feel someone standing behind me, massaging my neck. One might think that, as a homie once said to me, it's a "fragment of my imagination." But I know, like one knows such things, it is my father, even though he's been dead for ten years. I feel the thumbs digging into the sinews of my neck, right into the area most affected by these old fear-filled storylines. And I'll be damned: Fitch shampoo and Aqua Velva. I cry, as only one can after having been massaged into a new-found sense of sacred presence, deepened peace, and an unshakable holy assurance.[10]

The healing touch of God reaches out to us when we are open and most in need, mending our hearts and renewing our faith. The Spirit of God is mysterious, like the wind, Jesus told Nicodemus (John 3). We cannot create the wind; we cannot control the wind. All we can do is set up the sails of our lives, so that when that mysterious wind sweeps into our lives, we will be able to receive it and allow our lives to be nurtured by grace. Prayerfully engaging in the steps of forgiveness is our way of setting up the sails to receive the healing wind of the Spirit. "We set the sails, but it is God who sends the wind" (St. Augustine).

# SPIRITUAL EXERCISES AND PERSONAL REFLECTIONS

## A. A Poetic Reflection: I Am[11]

I was regretting the past
and fearing the future.
Suddenly my Lord was speaking:
My name is I AM.
When you live in the past,
with its mistakes and regrets,
it is hard. I am not there.
My name is not I Was.
When you live in the future,
with its problems and fears,
it is hard. I am not there.
My name is not I Will Be.
When you live in this moment,
it is not hard. I am here.
My name is I AM.

## B. Personal Reflection: Dealing with Regrets Consciously

When we find ourselves lost in regrets in such a way that it adversely affects our perspective on life, clarifying what is bothering us and deciding what we can do about it can save us from drowning in a pool of regret. A helpful process entails answering the following questions:

1. What is the problem? Name the specific regret.
2. How is it affecting me?
3. What *can* I do about it?
4. What do I *want* to do about it?

# C. A Reflection Guide to Healing and Forgiveness

The following reflections are taken from a meditation composed by Herb K., a teacher, spiritual director, and author of *Practicing the Here and Now: Being Intentional with Step 11* (Hazelden Publishing, 2017). Because he has distilled the rich wisdom of twelve-step spirituality so succinctly and helpfully, we have adapted his meditation into a process guide for dealing with hurts, resentments, and forgiveness. This guide describes the different phases of the healing process and is not meant to be followed in any strict order or time frame. Its usage will depend on individuals and how they find the aspects of the meditation helpful, given their personal background and concrete circumstances.

> *Facing and Naming the Hurt*: Open your mind and heart to remember the hurts, the wounds; recall where and when you have been let down, dishonored, abused, lied to, cheated on, diminished—spiritually, emotionally, physically or financially.
>
> Let a picture of the person who harmed you or caused you deep pain freely surface in your memory and mind—your father or mother, husband or wife, a boyfriend or girlfriend, brother or sister, a relative or a friend. If you have been betrayed or hurt by your school, church, the judicial system, the healthcare system, the government, allow the picture of a concrete person who symbolizes the institution surface in your memory or mind.
>
> This is the reality—it did happen—we have been betrayed, hurt, and wounded. Name it and accept it. It is tragic and it is true.
>
> *What Forgiveness Entails*: It is also true that we can be healed from these wounds.

- To forgive is not to condone or excuse the behavior. What was done was wrong.
- To forgive is not to pardon or exonerate—that's not ours to give—we don't have the power to absolve.
- To forgive is not to forget. We are saddened by the memory and must grieve.
- To forgive is to release from debt; to release from the demand for retribution or retaliation.
- To forgive is to surrender the right to get even. The reality is that as long as we hold on to these hurts, they possess us and poison us emotionally and spiritually.
- To forgive is to take responsibility for our part, which may only be that we have been holding on to these memories and feelings, allowing them to continue to devastate our emotional and spiritual life.
- How long are we going to carry these wounds?
- How long are we going to be shackled by the chain that tows this garbage of hurt, resentment, and shame?

*Acknowledging Our Own Brokenness*: Look at our own brokenness—the pain and hurts for which we have been responsible.

Look at our motives and role in those events where we find ourselves being unfair or disloyal. Where were we selfish, dishonest, angry, or afraid?

*Acknowledging the Brokenness of Others*: In light of our own brokenness, look at *their* brokenness. See how they are like us. Those who have hurt us are themselves hurt, fearful, wounded, fragile, sick people—human beings twisted by their own personal histories.

We are all weak, wounded human beings, imperfect and full of defects—attempting to survive the difficulties of life and find a little peace and happiness.

*Willingness to Forgive*: Forgiveness is the release of others and the harm they have caused us. But forgiveness often follows deep acceptance of and repentance for our own harmful actions to others.

## Acknowledging Our Powerlessness and Need for Healing Grace:

We often feel powerless to name and accept the truth of the harm we have done. We likewise feel powerless to release the hurt others have done to us. This is especially true when dealing with deep pain. "Though the decision to forgive must always come from within, we cannot change on our own strength. The power of forgiveness comes not from us, but from God. [God] can work in us only when we turn to [God] in prayer, trust, and humble recognition of our weaknesses."[12]

Am I willing to pray for the power:

- To ask for knowledge of the truth?
- To ask for freedom from the bondage of my own history?
- To wish for the spiritual healing of those persons or institutions that have harmed me?
- To forgive myself—to let go of self-condemnation, to let go of remorse, our temper, our addictions, our vanities, our arrogance, our smugness; to let go of our failures to do what we must and be who we are?

Am I willing to pray for the power:

- To love those who have hurt me as I love myself?
- To see the world and the people in it through the eyes of divine compassion?
*Prayer*: Inviting the healing power of God

# AGING WITH WISDOM AND GRACE

- Into our minds—that our memories may be healed;
- Into our hearts—that our feelings may be healed;
- Into our souls—that our spirit may be healed and may flourish.

We pray to the healing Spirit in the universe:

- Enable me to be willing to let go, to forgive, to release
- Enable me to be willing to find freedom
- Enable me to be willing to be restored to sanity
- Enable me to be willing to be taken to a place of serenity.

Holy Spirit, enter the recesses of my heart, mind, and soul and remove all traces of bitterness, anger and resentment. Free me from feelings and grudges that steal my energy and rob me of peace. Fill me with gratefulness for your merciful love and help me to be an instrument of your healing and forgiveness. AMEN.

# Chapter 7

# STAYING ENGAGED

At the core, life is not about things, it is about relationships. It is the hands we go on holding in our hearts at the end that define the kind of life we have led.

—Joan Chittister, *The Gift of Years*

Retirement is ranked tenth on the list of life's forty-three most stressful events.[1] This is easy to understand since retirement is a life transition that involves changes in surroundings, social interactions, and daily routines. For those whose work is a major source of purpose, retirement brings a shift in identity, self-worth, and connection with others. It is not uncommon to hear recent retirees complain of feeling bored, isolated, or down. Unstructured time and a slower pace of life can be disconcerting for both men and women and cause us to doubt our worth, now that we are no longer busy earning a paycheck or raising a family. While retirement affects people differently, for everyone it represents a milestone in life that challenges us to establish a new social network and find opportunities to continue to use our gifts and skills in ways that are personally rewarding and of benefit to others.

# AGING WITH WISDOM AND GRACE

A friend who retired a year ago spoke honestly about the difficulty he was having adjusting to "his new state in life." Having looked forward to retirement for many years, he now found himself lost and feeling like a man without a country. When he ran into people at the grocery store or in the neighborhood and they would ask, "What's new?" or "What have you been doing lately?" he didn't know what to say. In social situations, when asked what he did for a living, he hated having to say, "I'm retired," because it made him feel diminished. For twenty-five years he had been a judge. People knew who he was and, in the courtroom, he was in charge. He belonged. He had work friends and acquaintances, and, most importantly, he had self-respect. His wife used to enjoy it when he took the occasional day off. Lately, she seemed annoyed to have him around all the time and even told him, "I married you for life, not for lunch!"

Productivity is the coin of the realm in American society and determines how others judge our value—and sometimes how we judge ourselves. We are obsessed with being productive and preoccupied with working *harder, better, and faster*. Apple's app store and Google Play have an entire category devoted to productivity tools that promise to maximize output—"time management," "peak performance periods," "efficiency skills," "optimal work flow," "work smarter, not harder," to name just a few. Companies reward workers who go above and beyond expectations with generous bonuses. Underlying the emphasis on tangible results is the idea that our time and efforts must have something to show for themselves to be considered important. But productivity, as measured by outcomes that can be monetized, naturally declines when we retire. And overnight that which has given us meaning and purpose for the past thirty or forty years is gone and can leave us struggling with our identity and worth.

Most people come to retirement unprepared for the emotional and psychological issues that it brings. But quickly they discover that they need more than a healthy nest egg to make them happy.

Having looked forward to retirement, even idealizing it as utopia, they're surprised by the feeling of being useless. Swedish gerontologist Lars Tornstam sees this as the dark side of our cultural fixation with results-oriented productivity. He urges us, instead, to broaden our understanding of productivity to include activities that are nonmaterial, less ego driven, and not motivated by "what's in it for me." His theory of gerotranscendence focuses on fruitfulness or generativity—giving back and contributing to the welfare of others—as a vital source of meaning for older adults who still have much to offer. He rejects negative stereotypes of old age, such as being "over the hill," which devalue the rich contributions that the older generation can make to society. The fact that we are living longer has given birth to a new conception of aging that, in the words of psychologist Louis Colozino, "incorporates...traditional, non-economic contributions to the family" and "requires revised myths, new heroes and heroines, and stories of wise and compassionate elders who are available, loving and nurturing....Our increased longevity, hard-won wisdom and deeper self-awareness are resources we can invest in others."[2] One of the keys to thriving in our postretirement years is maintaining a healthy sense of self-worth that stems from the knowledge that we have the capacity to enrich the lives of others.

# Being Productive, Being Fruitful

During our working years, productivity sets the pace and tone of our days; we face regular performance reviews covering such things as meeting sales quotas, billable hours, student evaluations, number of publications, research grants, etcetera. When productivity dominates our lives, values such as leisure, quality time with family and friends, exercise and rest tend to take a back seat. We think that we will find more time for these things next month, or next year when the pressure is off, but that time never comes because one deadline replaces another.

Fruitfulness, in contrast to productivity, creates a different way of living—a slower pace that allows us time to relax and savor what is around us in the moment. We are able to live in the present, not preoccupied with measurable results or asking ourselves, "What's the *use* of what I'm doing?" Usefulness has nothing to do with the joy of being with loved ones, delighting in a sunset, being enthralled by a book or a piece of music; such moments are rewarding in themselves. "There are no awards for planting gardens, or playing with our grandchildren, or taking stock of our lives, no social 'payback' for practicing mindfulness, becoming conscious of our fears, unloosing the mental knot of lifetimes spent striving and achieving."[3] Such moments may be "useless" or "unproductive" in economic terms, but they are rich in satisfaction and fulfillment.

# Being Generous and Generative

While productivity relates to our work and what we do, fruitfulness relates to the kind of person we are and the quality of our life. We are fruitful and generative when those around us experience our presence to be nurturing and affirming. Being engaged and involved taps into our human need to enhance the life of others, especially those of upcoming generations. When we lose the sense that we can make a difference in the lives of others, we feel worthless.

Anglican priest George Herbert describes the sadness of feeling impotent or useless and the joy that comes when a sense of fruitfulness is revived. A captive to illness and depression for most of his life, Herbert struggled terribly with a lingering sense of his own worthlessness. Confessing to God his bewilderment and anxiety about being of no value to anyone, he prayed,

## Staying Engaged

What thou wilt do with me
None of my books will show:
I read, and sigh, and wish I were a tree;
For sure then I should grow
To fruit or shade; at least some bird would trust
Her household to me.[4]

His prayer changes to feelings of joy when his sense of vitality and creativity returns.

How fresh, Oh Lord, how sweet and clean
Are thy returns!...

Who would have thought my shrivel'd heart
Could have recover'd greenness?...

And now in age I bud again,
After so many deaths I live and write;
I once more smell the dew and rain,
And relish versing: Oh my only light,
It cannot be
That I am he
On whom thy tempests fell at night.[5]

It is not hard for those who have had times of feeling useless to resonate with Herbert's sadness. The antidote for feeling unneeded, unwanted, and useless is to seek ways of contributing to community, family, and neighbors by volunteering in whatever way is needed. The experience of grandparenting also brings satisfaction and joy because "the enthusiastic love of grandchildren and their insatiable need for interaction and attention come untainted by the prejudice of ageism."[6] "What a bargain grandchildren are!" exclaimed Gene Perret. "I give them my loose change, and they give me a million dollars' worth of pleasure."[7] Taking care of grandchildren is fulfilling because it makes us feel appreciated. It gives us the opportunity for more contact with our adult children as well as a chance to contribute to the family and to play at the same time! The feelings of a fifty-two-year-old grandmother of a pregnant teenager and three little boys capture how caring for the young can be life-giving and fulfilling.

> I have been diagnosed with cancer three times. I'm on chemotherapy now. Do you know that raising these kids and receiving their love is what keeps me alive? Believe it! I'm not going anywhere until they are grown and have their own families. By then I'll be raising another group of kids. It will be my third time around. I thank God for the chance.[8]

For older adults, "grandparenting, mentoring, and contributing to the lives of others may be as important as loving touch is for a young child."[9]

# Staying Connected: Key to Ongoing Vitality

A neuroscientific perspective on the aging brain places increased importance on staying connected and engaged with others. "Stimulation, challenge, and being needed by others," states neuropsychologist Cozolino, "tell the brain to be alert, learn new things and stay in shape." In contrast, the "lack of stimulation, repetitive routines, and isolation...runs the risk of sending our brain the message that they no longer need to grow."[10] Key to ongoing health and longevity, he says, is "being with others and staying engaged in taking on the challenges of life that builds, shapes, and sustains our brain."[11] The brain as a social organ survives and thrives through stimulating interactions with others.

The amount of unstructured time that is part of old age can be a source of loneliness and isolation. According to the Health and Retirement Study, about 28 percent of older Americans feel chronically lonely.[12] In 2016, the U.S. Surgeon General sounded a warning that Americans are "facing an epidemic of loneliness and social isolation."[13] Going beyond emotional distress, chronic loneliness also has corrosive health effects. Researchers report that "people, who routinely feel lonely or cut off from friends and family are more likely to suffer high blood pressure, develop heart disease and be diagnosed with dementia." They are also more likely to see their function decline as they age and are 50 percent more likely to die prematurely.[14]

The spiritual challenge in times of loneliness is the transformation of loneliness into solitude. The primary experience of loneliness is self-alienation—being disconnected from oneself. One feels confused and doesn't understand what's going on in the swirl of fluctuating thoughts and emotions. In contrast, solitude creates a free and friendly space that allows us to pay attention to what's going on in us without outside distractions. Chiming in on a conversation between his parents about the importance of solitude, a precocious fourth grader surprised them with a graphic description. "Is solitude like," he asked, "when I go to my room, close the door, sit on my bed and the outside noises like the banging of the pots in the kitchen get smaller and the inside noises get bigger?"

Loneliness, which alienates us from ourselves, also keeps us from connecting closely to others, even when we are with them. Relationships that never get beyond the superficial end up being dull and unsatisfying. It is the self-knowledge we gain in solitude that expands our capacity to relate more intimately with others. Knowing what is going on in our inner life makes intimate sharing possible. A teenager who was feeling pressured by his parents to share what was going on in his life retorted, "Let me get back to you when I hear from myself!" When we do not "hear" from ourselves, what we share will lack genuineness and depth. Solitude contributes to graceful aging by making us more able to engage personally with family and friends. As Jung once observed, "Loneliness does not come from having no people around, but from being unable to communicate the things that seem important to oneself."

Solitude is time alone for the sake of connecting with our inner life—our thoughts and feelings, anxieties and fears, desires and frustrations, hopes and longings. Aging provides many natural opportunities for turning inward. We need to build into our lives time to "consider our deepest questions about who we are, where we are, and how it all makes sense," advises Ram Dass. "It is a great feeling to be able to open the door to mystery and reflect on the deeper significance of life. Slowing down is the only way to take advantage of this opportunity."[15]

# Giving Life through Caring Presence

While a commitment to living generously and generatively is lofty, the manner of doing so is ordinary. Jean Vanier, the founder of a community dedicated to helping men and women with mental disabilities, put it quite simply:

> I think all we're called to do is little things, but little things with love—little things of simplicity and humility. To live today in our family with our husband and wife and children and love them, to love them really and to be open to the neighbors, the little old lady down the road who has no friends....[16]

Each of us is presented daily with opportunities to be a life-giving presence to others. Being there for others does not require any special training or course of study. It requires only that we listen sensitively and compassionately to them.

***Listening:*** Simply listening with care is a way of being loving and nurturing. Many people experience the pain of not having anyone in their lives who will listen to them in an empathic and nonjudgmental way. They want to communicate, but experience over and over that no one wants to listen. No wonder we hear the same people repeat the same complaints, the same stories for months and years! Listening with care is simply being there and allowing our heart to be touched, like the child in the following story:

> One day a woman's little girl arrived home late after school. The mother was so angry that she started to yell at her. However, after about five minutes, she suddenly stopped and asked: "Why are you so late anyway?"
>
> The daughter replied: "Because I had to help another girl who was in trouble."
>
> "Well, what did you do to help her?"
>
> The daughter replied, "Oh, I sat down next to her and helped her cry."[17]

This young girl models a way of caring that older adults, free from the pressures of job and other responsibilities, are well positioned to do. No wonder grandparents are often the go-to persons for people weighed down with worries. To listen in a way that is generative does not require professional expertise, because the emphasis here is on caring, not curing. When we feel responsible for curing others, we slip into wanting to fix, protect, rescue, and control. Preoccupied with finding a solution, we end up not listening. Conversely, when we are mainly concerned with showing care, we can listen with sensitivity and understanding.

> From experience you know that those who care for you become present to you. When they speak, they speak to you. And when they ask questions, you know it is for your sake and not for their own. Their presence is a healing presence, because they accept you on your terms,

> and they encourage you to take your own life seriously
> and to trust your own vocation.[18]

Listening reaches its maximum potential for healing when the pain of others is truly perceived; when we understand the pain behind the words, the hurt behind the anger, the fears behind the aggressiveness, the insecurity behind the rigidity. To simply hear it all—without judging, evaluating, minimizing, or fixing—makes our presence truly nurturing and supportive.

*Affirming:* Our caring presence must also affirm others' ability to take responsibility for their own lives and to rely on their own inner strength and resources to make decisions and changes. To affirm is to say to another, "You can do it!" It requires that we resist carrying those who can walk and instead say "get up and walk," as Jesus said to the paralytic who had been waiting for a cure for thirty-eight years. Jesus's words awakened his deep desire to be whole again and stirred him into action to make a change (see John 5:1–9). Those who feel paralyzed and helpless may simply need our encouragement and support to believe in themselves again.

When people feel stuck or helpless, we can help them to imagine new possibilities. Imagining with others alleviates their loneliness and stimulates their creativity. Our ability to imagine alternatives is greater when doing it with others, as the technique of brainstorming illustrates. In organizations, for example, creative problem solving is enhanced when done in a supportive group. Hope is born when people can imagine how things can be other than they are. And energy flows when they find themselves committed to making what they see in their imagination a concrete reality in their life.

Even in less than ideal situations, we can use our own imagination to find ways of helping others. The following story is a good example of the creative use of one's imagination in the service of another:

## Staying Engaged

Two men, both seriously ill, occupied the same hospital room. One man was allowed to sit up in his bed for an hour each afternoon to help drain the fluid from his lungs. His bed was next to the room's only window. The other man had to spend all his time flat on his back.

The men talked for hours on end. They spoke of their wives and families, their homes, their jobs, their involvement in the military service, where they had been on vacation.

And every afternoon when the man in the bed by the window could sit up, he would pass the time by describing to his roommate all things he could see outside the window. The man in the other bed began to live for those one-hour periods when his world would be broadened and enlivened by all the activity and color of the world outside.

The window overlooked a park with a lovely lake. Ducks and swans played on the water while children sailed their model boats. Young lovers walked arm in arm amidst flowers of every color of the rainbow. Grand old trees graced the landscape, and a fine view of the city skyline could be seen in the distance.

As the man by the window described all this in exquisite detail, the man on the other side of the room would close his eyes and imagine the picturesque scene.

One afternoon the man by the window described a parade passing by. Although the other man couldn't hear the band, he could see it in his mind's eyes as the gentleman by the window portrayed it with descriptive words.

Days and weeks passed. One morning, the day nurse arrived to bring water for their bath only to find the lifeless body of the man by the window, who had died peacefully in his sleep. She was saddened and called the hospital attendant to take the body away.

As soon as it seemed appropriate, the other man asked if he could be moved next to the window. The nurse was happy to make the switch and after making sure he was comfortable, she left him alone. Slowly, painfully, he propped himself up on one elbow to take his first look at the world outside. Finally, he would have the joy of seeing it for himself. He strained to slowly turn to look out the window beside the bed. It faced a wall.

The man asked the nurse what could have compelled his deceased roommate who had described such wonderful things outside the window. The nurse responded that the man was blind and could not even see the wall. She said, "Perhaps he just wanted to encourage you."

*Attributed to Harry Buschman*

# Making Ourselves Available

"God has put you in my path" (*Dios te puso en mi camino*) is a common saying among Latinos. It reminds us that God's loving care for those in need often depends on our willingness to embody God's care in a tangible way. To know that God counts on us is to live with a sense of personal significance. Ordinary acts, such as listening and affirming, make a difference in the lives of those who yearn for companionship and support. Through our simple actions, they can experience the intimate touch of God.

That each of us is important in the divine scheme of things is a message nicely nestled in the story of Joseph and how he ended up in Egypt due to his brothers' treachery (Gen 37—41). Commenting on the story, Rabbi Lawrence Kushner illustrates how significant a single person's contribution to God's plan can be and how highly we must regard our calling to be instruments in the hands of the Most High.[19]

Having been sent by his father to check on his brothers who were supposed to be tending the flocks in Shechem, Joseph discovered upon arrival that they were not there. "A man (*ish*) found him wandering in the fields; the man asked him, 'What are you seeking?' 'I am seeking my brothers,' he said; 'tell me, please, where they are pasturing the flock.' The man said, 'They have gone away, for I heard them say, "Let us go to Dothan."'" So Joseph went after his brothers, and found them at Dothan" (Gen 37:15–17).

Kushner suggests that the "man" (*ish*) was a messenger and that his passing exchange with Joseph was full of divine purpose. One of the greatest events in the salvation history of the Jews (the exodus from Egypt) might not have happened if it were not for the part played by *ish*. "Indeed were it not for the man who 'happened' to find Joseph wandering in the field," writes Kushner, "he would have returned home. Never been sold into slavery. Never brought his family down to Egypt. The Jewish people would never become slaves. And indeed there could have been no Jewish people at all."[20] Known only by his deed of giving Joseph directions that were crucial to his finding his brothers, he remains nameless. His name is quite secondary to the simple task he was sent to perform. The Torah only calls him *ish*, "someone." Yet without him, the great deeds that God did for the children of Israel would never have occurred.

The significance of *ish* unfolds in the final chapters of Genesis, which tell the story of Joseph, a favored and spoiled son. Joseph's grandiose dreams of being set over his brothers in a privileged position provoked their wrath, just as his being their father's favorite evoked their envy. When an opportunity arose, his brothers sold him to a caravan of traders headed for Egypt and what they hoped would be oblivion. Joseph's gift as a dream interpreter, however, eventually made the Pharaoh elevate him to second-in-command of the realm, giving Joseph such power that he was able to manipulate situations so that his eleven brothers, along with their father, could escape a famine by settling in Egypt.

"Clearly, the Torah means to teach us that it is all the doing of the Holy One," states Rabbi Kushner. "Event after event has the unmistakable mark of divine contrivance. But of all these scenes chronicling our descent into Egypt, none seems more superfluous and dramatically unnecessary than the scene in Shechem."[21] The story of *ish* highlights the importance of being open and available to being used by the Creator of the universe to contribute to life.

# God Counts on Everyone: The Story of *Ish*

Every one of us is an *ish*, a "someone." No more and no less than the unnamed stranger of the empty pastures of Shechem, whose simple assistance to a perplexed Joseph allowed God's purpose to be accomplished. Even in the afternoon of life, we are called, no matter our age, to give the living God a face that others can see. What we do for others may seem small and unimportant, yet even our simple efforts count. As Martin Luther King Jr. once put it, "Life's most persistent and urgent question is, 'What are you doing for others?'" Desiring to be a tangible extension of God's loving touch to others, St. Francis Assisi prayed,

> Lord, make me an instrument of your peace!
> Where there is hatred, let me sow love;
> Where there is injury, pardon;
> Where there is doubt, faith;
> Where there is despair, hope;
> Where there is darkness, light;
> Where there is sadness, joy.
> O divine master,

## Staying Engaged

Grant that I may not so much seek to be
Consoled as to console,
To be understood as to understand,
To be loved as to love.
For it is in giving that we receive,
It is in pardoning that we are pardoned,
And it is in dying
That we are born to eternal life.

(Prayer of St. Francis)[22]

# SPIRITUAL EXERCISES AND PERSONAL REFLECTIONS

## A. Reflection Questions

1. For what are you most grateful at this time in your life?
2. How does your gratitude find expression in your response to others?
3. Where in your life are you being called to contribute to the lives of others by sharing your presence and gifts?

## B. Loving in a Way That Bears Fruit

**Fall in Love[23]**

Nothing is more practical than
finding God, than
falling in Love
in a quite absolute, final way.
What you are in love with,
what seizes your imagination, will affect everything.
It will decide
what will get you out of bed in the morning,
what you do with your evenings,
how you spend your weekends,
what you read, whom you know,
what breaks your heart,
and what amazes you with joy and gratitude.
Fall in love, stay in love
and it will decide everything.

# Chapter 8

# BEING GRATEFUL

For all that has been, thanks,
For all that will be, yes.

—Dag Hammarskjold

Why is it that some people are crabbier and more disgruntled as they grow old, while others, living in similar circumstances, are more positive and content? After spending a year with the oldest of the old, Leland, to his surprise, discovered that life circumstances were not as important as one's perspective on life when it came to being happy. He found that those who were most content in their old age viewed life as a gift and were grateful, while those who resented growing old focused on their losses and ailments. "How," he wonders, "would things be different if instead of thinking of late life as getting old, we thought of it as living long—a gift given those lucky enough to be born in the right century?"[1]

Sometimes a simple shift in outlook is all it takes for us to see the blessings in our life that we easily overlook when we focus on what displeases us. The following story illustrates this. One day, a disciple complained to the master,

"I am in desperate need of help—or I'll go crazy. We're living in a single room—my wife, my children and my in-laws. So our nerves are on edge, we yell and scream at one another. The room is a hell."

"Do you promise to do whatever I tell you?" said the Master gravely.

"I swear I shall do anything."

"Very well. How many animals do you have?"

"A cow, a goat and six chickens."

"Take them all into the room with you. Then come back after a week."

The disciple was appalled. But he had promised to obey! So he took the animals in. A week later he came back, a pitiable figure, moaning, "I'm a nervous wreck. The dirt! The stench! The noise! We're all on the verge of madness!"

"Go back," said the Master, "and put the animals out."

The man ran all the way home. And came back the following day, his eyes sparkling with joy.

"How sweet life is! The animals are out. The home is a Paradise—so quiet and clean and roomy."[2]

When we accept that life is made up of both hardships and blessings, we are able to appreciate and enjoy the life we have. "We do ourselves a big favor not to be scared of growing old," writes Leland, "but to embrace the mixed bag that the years have to offer, however severe the losses."[3]

# Gratitude as a Pathway to Graceful Aging

The findings of psychology can often come as no great surprise, since they validate what we already know from our own experience. This is particularly true of studies that show a strong correlation between being happy and being grateful. That people who are grateful tend to be happier than those who are not is not surprising. And while gratitude is important no matter how old a person is, it is key to flourishing in old age when accumulated losses and fears about the future pile up.

Gratitude is also good for our health. A number of studies suggest that people who are grateful tend to experience fewer symptoms of physical illness than those who are not grateful. As an example, feeling grateful to God reduces the adverse effects of stress on the health of older people.[4] According to the findings of the Harvard Study of Adult Development, gratitude also has a noticeable impact on our emotional well-being. Psychiatrist George Vaillant, in his *Aging Well*, which is based on the Harvard Study, suggests that those who are most satisfied and well adjusted in their older years are those who worry less about gray hairs and waistlines and more about gratitude and forgiveness.

We witnessed this in our own family with Marion Olsen, who at ninety-nine exuded a vibrancy and love for life that endeared her to all who knew her. At Christmas one year, when we told her we were writing a book on gratitude, she lit up and shared with us how wonderful her life had been and how grateful she felt for all she had been given. When we asked her if she would compile a gratitude list that we could include in our book, she agreed, and two weeks later, we received the following letter:

> The longer I live, the more I find to be grateful for. Every day is a gift, and I'm grateful that I am aware of it. I'm grateful for:
>
> - An especially good sleep last night
> - Being able to remember something different everyday
> - The loving attention of my family
> - Being able to tie my own shoes

- My 20/20 vision (with glasses!)
- My appetite for life
- My wonderful dentist
- Being able to manicure my own fingernails
- Remembering who gave me which gifts
- My taste buds
- Getting to the bathroom on time!

We have no doubt that Marion's grateful attitude was the key to her joy in living. Until her death at age 106, she would often say, "Isn't life wonderful!" From Marion, we learned that a grateful attitude can ease many of the burdens of aging and enable us to thrive, no matter what life throws at us.

# Focusing on the Positives

Henry Miller once commented, "At eighty I believe I am a far more cheerful person than I was at twenty or thirty." No Pollyanna, Miller's attitude might be explained by what researchers call the positivity effect. "Experience helps older people moderate their expectations and makes them more resilient when things don't go as hoped," notes Leland in his observations of the oldest old. "When they do have negative experiences, they don't dwell on them as much as younger people do."[5] Maintaining an attitude of gratitude requires a willingness to view life with appreciation. It involves a conscious choice, an antecedent predisposition, to see the glass as half full rather than half empty. When we focus on the positives, we keep our eyes on what we *have* rather than what we *don't have*.

Comparing our situation to those who are less fortunate, what psychologists refer to as "downward comparison," is a simple exercise that helps us to maintain an appreciation of what is good in our lives. Seeing a homeless person, for example, can evoke appreciation for having a roof over our head; the disappointment at not being promoted can be mitigated by hearing that a colleague was let go. In contrast, "upward comparison," when we compare ourselves to those we think have it better than we do, makes us feel envious and resentful. Instead of counting our own blessings and appreciating what we have, we start counting other people's blessings and devaluing our own. For those of us who tend to see the glass as half empty, downward comparison can get us back on track.

# The Struggle to Be Grateful

Are some people more prone to being grateful than others? Research on gratitude suggests that the answer is yes, that our genetic makeup disposes some of us to see the dark, rather than the bright, side of life. Genetics, however, is only half of the story; the other half has to do with life circumstances and intentional activities we engage in that influence our moods and attitudes. Specifically, our genes are 50 percent responsible, our life circumstances 10 percent, while the rest, 40 percent, is due to our personal choices. In other words, gratitude is a choice that we can make, no matter our past or present circumstances. "Of course," we think, "it's easy for people to be grateful when they have everything they want—good health, great relationships, and a secure retirement nest egg." But as we know, there are people who have suffered terrible losses and had more than their share of setbacks and heartaches and still manage to be grateful despite it all. The realization that it is our attitude toward life, and not our life circumstances, that determines how happy or unhappy we are is good news, especially as we encounter the inevitable ailments and losses that come with aging. The truth of this was brought home to Leland during the many conversations he had with the "oldest old."

...all found a level of happiness not in their external circumstance, but in something they carried with them. No one wants to lose his partner of sixty years or to give up walking because it hurts too much, but we have some choice in how we process the loss and the life left to us. We can focus on what we've lost or on the life we have now. Health factors, as shattering as they can be, are only part of the story."[6]

Brother David Steindl-Rast, who is renowned for his spirituality of gratefulness, believes that it is not happiness that causes gratitude, but rather gratitude is the key to happiness.

# Cultivating Gratitude

Sometimes a simple practice can help expand our gratitude and alter debilitating moods. In describing herself as a recovering pessimist, Karen Reivich, PhD, a research associate at the University of Pennsylvania, states, "Part of my brain is always scanning the horizon for danger." Instead of dismissing her concerns as unwarranted, Reivich created a simple practice to help herself to counter the dour, gloomy part of her personality. "I've created an 'awe wall' covered with poems, my children's photos, a picture of a lavender farm," she shares. "And every day I work on it a bit. I may add a cartoon that made me laugh and a picture drawn by my young son. It's hard to be basking in all these reminders of wonder and simultaneously be filled with dread." Strategies like these, when employed consistently over time, lead to long-lasting change. Reivich discovered that gradually her pessimistic habits started to atrophy.

At first the change happens at the surface, in a conscious change in behavior; then it begins to take place more deeply, becoming almost effortless. That's because I'm repeating the exercise until it becomes a new habit. If I focus my attention on noting good and thinking about the things I can control, I'm using my attention and energy to build optimism and happiness rather than to deepen worry and sadness.[7]

Deepening our appreciation for what we have is an important step in cultivating and sustaining gratitude. The popular saying "familiarity breeds contempt" points to the fact that our appreciation for things diminishes as we get used to them. What psychologists call "the law of habituation" reflects the human tendency to begin to take for granted that which we once treasured. This applies to material possessions, relationships, natural beauty, even our hard-earned successes and triumphs over adversity. In time, the extraordinary becomes ordinary and what once was a source of joy and gratitude becomes ho-hum. Renewing our sense of appreciation is a way of working against the law of habituation, because it increases our feelings of gratitude.

Fostering appreciation begins with expanding a sense of wonder, with seeing commonly taken-for-granted things with fresh eyes, as Patricia Schneider's poem, "The Patience of Ordinary Things" delightfully illustrates:

It is a kind of love, is it not?
How the cup holds the tea,
How the chair stands sturdy and foursquare,
How the floor receives the bottoms of shoes or toes.
How soles of feet know where they're supposed to be.
I've been thinking about the patience of ordinary
    things,
How clothes wait respectfully in closets
And soap dries quietly in the dish,
And towels drink the wet from the skin of the back.
And the lovely repetition of stairs.
And what is more generous than a window?[8]

Gazing with wonder at all of creation entails delighting in everyday things. Our gratitude expands when we view ordinary things with appreciative eyes. An appreciative posture can take the form of standing in awe before the dazzling colors of a rose garden or the majestic shape of trees lit up by the glow of a sunset; it can occur when marveling over the beauty of a clear blue sky. An amusing illustration of this kind of appreciative gaze is the incident recounted in Nikos Kazantzakis's *Zorba the Greek*: One day, Zorba was riding on a donkey with his boss. As they passed an oncoming traveler on another donkey, Zorba's eyes were fixed on the stranger. When chided by his companion for gawking so rudely at someone, Zorba proclaimed with childlike simplicity his amazement that there are such things as asses! Alexis Zorba's stance of amazement before daily realities, hardly noticed by most people, impressed his friend and narrator of the novel:

> I felt, as I listened to Zorba, that the world was recovering its pristine freshness. All the dulled daily things regained the brightness they had in the beginning, when we came out of the hands of God. Water, women, the stars, bread, returned to their mysterious, primitive origin and the divine whirlwind burst once more upon the air.[9]

To view ordinary things with astonishment—as if seeing them for the first time—broadens our capacity for appreciation and gratitude. This kind of lively wonder comes naturally to children and is something too soon lost on adults. Yet practice can rekindle wonder, even as we age.

# Gratitude Practices

Fostering a disposition of gratitude entails the regular use of practices that can keep us alert and aware of the blessings and gifts of ordinary life. Concrete practices—whether done daily, weekly, or monthly—keep us from taking things for granted. For example, just taking time out to record the things we are thankful for in a daily gratitude journal has the effect of sharpening our perception of good things that occur and deepening our appreciation. Simple practices such as those suggested below can easily become part of daily life.

***Breathing with Gratitude***: Occasionally throughout the day, slow down to pay attention to your breathing. Notice how this vital process of inhaling and exhaling happens so naturally, sustaining our aliveness moment by moment. Our appreciation for being able to breathe easily heightens when we compare our ease with people suffering from asthma or emphysema, who struggle for every breath. Let your attention to your breathing remind you of the blessing of being alive and well. Let it stir up feelings of gratitude to God who is the Author of our every breath. Denise Levertov beautifully describes God's love that sustains us in life from moment to moment in her poem "Primary Wonder."

> And then
> once more the quiet mystery
> is present to me, the throng's clamor
> recedes: the mystery
> that there is anything, anything at all,
> let alone cosmos, joy, memory, everything
> rather than void: and that, O Lord,
> Creator, Hallowed One, You still
> hour by hour sustain it.[10]

***Reliving a Blessed Moment of the Day***: Before retiring at night, briefly scan the activities and happenings, encounters and conversations you experienced that day. What brought you a moment of joy, excitement, pleasure, comfort, or sense of well-being? These can be simple things we often take for granted: a morning cup of coffee in quiet solitude or with someone we feel close to; a kindness extended to us by a stranger at the supermarket; a phone conversation that reconnected us with someone we miss; a kind word of concern or reassurance from a neighbor; a surprise email from a friend who has moved away.

Focus on just one such gratitude-evoking experience. In your memory and imagination, recall and relive that moment, letting your appreciation and gratitude for it deepen. This kind of gratitude review can surprise us with how often we let small, but significant, blessings slip through the cracks, not allowing them to fuel gratefulness in our hearts.

***Recalling Our Blessings Regularly***: Because of the human tendency to become used to things we enjoy and to take them for granted, it is important to call them to mind regularly. The British writer G. K. Chesterton suggests a way of regularly recalling our blessings by extending the practice of "saying grace before meals" to include other events of our day. He states, "You say grace before meals. All right. But I say grace before the concert and the opera, and grace before the play and pantomime, and grace before I open a book, and grace before sketching, painting, swimming, fencing, boxing, walking, playing, dancing and grace before I dip the pen in the ink."[11] Chesterton's practice of saying grace continually throughout the day invites us to consider how we might recall our blessings regularly. Prayers of thanksgiving can be formal ones that we have learned, like a traditional grace before meals, or an informal one that springs spontaneously from our heart.

***Writing a Gratitude Letter***: Another practice, one that psychiatrist Irvin Yalom has found especially effective, entails writing a gratitude letter and making a gratitude visit.

Think of someone still living toward whom you feel great gratitude that you have never expressed. Spend ten minutes writing that person a gratitude letter....The final step is that you pay a personal visit to that person sometime in the near future and read that letter aloud.[12]

***Recalling a Joyful Memory***: Another way to rekindle gratitude is to focus on joyful moments from the past. John Sorensen, at age ninety-one, provides two examples of this.

> I'll never forget coming into the living room once and my dad had a canary on his hand. And my mother was looking at him, and I will never forget the smile on her face. It was like a young girl falling in love. I never saw such a smile on my mother. It was only an instant, because as soon as they saw me it changed. But it was a beautiful memory that's engraved in my mind.[13]

Another time, he recalled,

> It was one of those God-given days, where everything just glowed. I remember the ocean was calm, and it just glittered like diamonds out there. At the end of the day my brother was visiting me, and I have pictures of the last time I saw him alive.[14]

Tapping into joyful memories begins with recalling scenes from your life when you felt deep love and profound joy: a celebration of a wedding, anniversary, a family holiday reunion, or a special birthday. Then dwell on one of these times and relive the events in memory; picture as concretely as you can the original setting, the faces of the people involved, and the emotions that you were feeling then. Recall who and what brought such joy. What did you hear or see that gave you delight? Lastly, reexperience as much as you can the love and joy you felt. This simple exercise brings the joys of the past into the present.

Gratitude, suggests psychologist Philip Watkins, plays an important role in our ability to recall positive experiences from our past. He found that those who are predisposed to being grateful tend to notice the good things that happen to them when they occur and that this enhances "the encoding of these experiences in memory."[15] In other words, another benefit of gratitude is that it not only enables us to appreciate favors we received in the moment they occur, but it also stores them more securely in our memory. Thus, he says, "Grateful individuals should be more likely to recall past benefits from their life and to experience gratitude in response to these blessings."[16] With poetic vividness, the following reflection captures what Watkins is talking about:

> Something seen, something heard, something felt, flashes upon one with a bright freshness, and the heart, tired or sick or sad or merely indifferent, stirs and lifts in answer. Different things do it for different people, but the result is the same: that fleeting instant when we lose ourselves in joy and wonder. It is minor because it is slight and so soon gone; it is an ecstasy because there is an impersonal quality in the vivid thrust of happiness we feel, and because the stir lingers in the memory.[17]

By enabling us to recall positive memories more easily, gratitude helps us to better cope with loss and diminishment. For example, when we suffer the death of loved ones—a painful aspect of aging—positive memories can be a source of comfort. "This is where memory helps," a writer on aging and spiritual growth states, "and why old people treasure it so much. It is a kind of hump in which we store recollections of happiness, of being loved, of people and places that were dear to us, of pleasure and success in work, of the joys of child-rearing."[18]

One of the blessings of growing older and slowing down is having the leisure to relish positive events in our life. Cistercian monk Basil Pennington described how he experienced this blessing of old age. As he got older, he found himself spending more time alone, but nevertheless felt the presence of loved ones who were "so present to the spirit, in the reality of memory, in the books of pictures I take out and leaf through. We are together again in wonderful moments of life," he stated. He found that past experiences could "be savored in a way that they could not be when they were rushing by in the midst of so many doings." When "the painful, the sad, the sorrowful memories" emerged, he chose "to 'flip the channel' and dwell with the memories" that he chose. Yet, he acknowledged that at times it was "consoling to hold again some painful memories, to hold them before God in healing and prayerful love."[19]

**Telling Our Story as a Grateful Tale**: When we recall the names, dates, and events that fill the seasons of our lives and put all that information into a narrative structure, we are telling our life story. We frame the facts of our life as a story in order to provide meaning and coherence to what would otherwise be a jumble of disconnected recollections. Looking back at our life in this way allows us to view our life as a meaningful whole, which psychologist Erick Erickson believes is an important late-in-life task. There are many ways we can tell our story. If, however, we tell it in a way that highlights how God has blessed us from our mother's womb, we cannot escape the fact that our lives have been "full of grace." Hence, an important gateway to increased gratitude is to tell our life story as one of grace.

We speak of grace here not in an abstract theological way, but as the concrete and tangible ways that the love of God has spilled into creation and flowed into our lives, sometimes in mysterious, but always in life-giving ways. Grace "includes unmerited favor, forgiveness, second-chances, surprises, reframings, epiphanic breakthroughs, whole paradigm shifts," a contemporary spiritual writer perceptively points out. "It is a word that reaffirms the gift character of all that we are and have. It is an organizing force in every life story."[20] By telling our story as a grace-filled tale, we intentionally focus our attention on all the people and events through which our lives have been touched by love and laced with the provident care of God.

With the lens of faith, we review our history with a keen eye focused on the myriad ways that we have been touched by grace. A prayerful look at our life helps us recognize in the ordinary course of our days the surprises and "unmerited gifts, the goodness that arises from the ash heap of failure, the joy that comes in the wake of loss, the times when God breaks through the logic of circumstances and ambushes us with love and with new opportunities."[21]

Telling our life story with the eyes of faith recounts how we experienced grace in daily life: for example, when a loved one forgives us for a wrong committed; when we are surprised by the steady support of faithful friends in the aftermath of a cancer diagnosis; or when we hear from a son or daughter from whom we have been estranged.

In a brief account of her own "salvation history," theologian Roberta Bond "dis-members" both the happy and painful memories of life and "re-members" them, weaving a story of her life as a tale of grace. As with the Israelites of old, God's faithfulness provides the unifying framework for her story. When she was a little girl, despair pervaded her, making her fear that even at age twenty-five she would never be "an ordinary, powerful, confident, self-sufficient, outgoing, competent grown-up who actually talked to other grown-ups."[22] And her childhood fears seemed to have come true, for at twenty-five, her experience of her life matched her worst fears.

> I didn't feel powerful; in fact, I hardly felt in control of my life at all. Whether I was pleasing my husband caused me great anxiety. I worried constantly about meeting other people's expectations and I sought their approval compulsively. I rarely experienced myself as competent. I continued to suffer from shyness as well as the dependent loneliness of childhood, and trying to talk to adults even a little older than I was excruciating.[23]

Yet years later, she was able to proclaim with grateful wonderment, "It would have seemed impossible then [at age twenty-five] that I should look back over my life from where I am now and not only know that it is a good thing to be fifty-five, but also be glad that there is no one on earth whose life I would trade for mine."[24]

In sharing how aging has been so much more wonderful than she thought it could be, Bondi recounts the many blessings of her life: "an exceptional husband who is my companion in every way," children, a mother, friends, and students whom she enjoys and loves and who reciprocate in kind. She also mentions the blessing that the women's movement has been for her in opening doors of opportunity for rich and rewarding engagement outside the home in meaningful work. But above and beyond anything else, what has enabled her to recount the story of her life as a grateful tale is the abiding love of God, something she "only had glimpses of in my twenties." In intimate terms, she shares what has made all the difference in the world for her:

> It is a knowledge of my own grounding in God who over the years has slowly, steadily freed me from both debilitating perfectionism and guilt, and from the energy-sapping burden of trying to please everybody I know in both my personal and professional lives. This grounding in God continues to give me the strength to discern, work, and suffer for what I myself value. At the same time, it has increasingly allowed me a space to confront and be confronted by my own wounds to my ability to love and receive love and to seek healing from God.[25]

# Memory Keeps God's Presence Alive

Remembering God's faithfulness to us in the past is an important way of staying hopeful in the present. When we forget how

# AGING WITH WISDOM AND GRACE

God has come through for us in the past, we are less able to trust that God is with us in the present. Because memory loss is a normal part of aging, a spiritual practice that involves periodically calling to mind God's concrete blessings in the unfolding of our life story is important for spiritual vitality. This can take the form of writing a faith or spiritual autobiography in which we recount the "stepping stones" that have led us to where we are in the present. The following are some helpful questions in telling the story of God's presence in our life:

- What have been significant events in my life?
- Who have been important people in my life?
- How have I experienced God in the different stages of my life and development?
- In what ways in my life have I experienced the giving and receiving of love, affirmation, forgiveness, healing, and freedom?
- What biblical images or stories reflect how God has been part of my life?

Before trying to put any order to these recollections, it is helpful to randomly jot down memories from childhood and recent years as they come to awareness. Later, these memories can be organized into a personal story of our life with God. This exercise will help us to get in touch with our faith history and recognize how God's presence weaves itself through the events of our lives. The ability to remember is an essential aspect of grateful living. It allows us to cherish important persons and significant events of the past and to prolong our appreciation of them in the present.

# PERSONAL REFLECTIONS AND SPIRITUAL EXERCISES

## A. A Life Review through the Prism of Gratitude

Sit quietly and recall someone from your past whose kindness and care touched your heart. Imagine yourself in conversation with that person. Tell them how blessed you feel for the gift of their presence in your life and what they have meant to you. Send your gratitude to them as if your hearts were connected. Thank them, and when you are finished with the conversation, say a warm goodbye. Say farewell to them as if you might never see them again, even in memory.

In an unhurried way, call into mind, one by one, people who have supported you: parents, grandparents, friends, lovers, ministers, teachers, classmates, and colleagues. Share with each of them how grateful you are for their kindness and care. When you feel satisfied that you have expressed your love and gratitude to them, say goodbye as if you might never be this way again.

Every time you encounter in prayerful memory those whom you care for with gratitude, the experience changes slightly as the conversation unfolds under the influence of grace and the parting becomes less a separation than a completion.

As this gratitude practice continues, expand your attention to include not only people but also moments from the past for which you feel grateful. Recall those events when you felt blessed or graced and relive them with gratitude. Thank God for them.[26]

# Chapter 9

# ALL SHALL BE WELL

The days of our life are seventy years,
or perhaps eighty, if we are strong...
they are soon gone....

So teach us to count our days
that we may gain a wise heart.

—Psalm 90:10;12

Woody Allen is quoted as saying, "I don't mind the thought of my dying. I just don't want to be there when it happens." Death itself is not what many of us fear; what concerns us more is the actual experience of dying. The older we get, the more frequently we wonder about the manner of our death. We would like a "happy death"—pain free, at peace, at home surrounded by family and loved ones. But the circumstances of our dying are outside of our control. Our curiosity about the actual process, at times tinged with anxiety, may account for the interest in near-death experiences. These stories relate the experience of people who were clinically dead for a brief time and then lived to relate what happened to them. A common element in their stories is that they were not alone, but were accompanied by "spirits," usually deceased relatives and friends. They also describe encountering a loving and warm presence that they called "the being of light." Although life-after-life accounts can ease our fears by shedding a positive light on death and dying, it is hard for us to fathom what is one of life's biggest unknowns. How are we to approach something that is a mystery? Can we ever know the unknowable? The answer is that we can, in a limited way, get a glimpse of what is behind the veil of mystery by looking at what Jesus taught his disciples when they asked the kinds of questions we ask.

The New Testament tells the story of Lazarus, the brother of Martha and Mary, who had a life-after-life experience. Unfortunately for us, he left no account of what the experience was like. Christian spirituality, however, can help us to enter into the mystery within and beyond human life through the use of our imagination. Through symbols (like the cross), images (like God as Father or Mother) or metaphors (like the parables of Jesus, "The Kingdom of God is like…"), we are helped to imagine what the mysteries of faith might mean. An eighty-year-old friend, sharing his thoughts about dying and what it might be like, admitted, "I don't know, but I'm a hopeful agnostic!" For him, dying is a mystery beyond his ability to fathom, yet his belief in God's goodness and mercy makes him hopeful that at the time of death, he will be pleasantly surprised.

Like near-death accounts, the parables of Jesus can provide a way of imagining what dying might entail. Jesus used parables to convey his teachings about things that go beyond direct, concrete knowledge. Parables are metaphorical explanations that shed light on one reality by comparing it to another. A metaphor means "to see as." For those who fear dying because, for example, they imagine coming face-to-face with a judging God, parables offer a different way of seeing, one that can alleviate fear. A central message of Jesus is that we need not fear, because we have a God who is loving and forgiving. To convey this message, he told three parables—the parable of the lost sheep, the lost coin, and the prodigal son (Luke 15)—that illustrate God's extravagant love for us, a love that goes beyond what we might imagine. Might these parables provide a lens for looking at the Christian understanding of dying as an encounter with a loving and forgiving God whom Jesus called "Abba," and who the risen Jesus said is also our Father? To Mary Magdalene, the first witness of the resurrection, Jesus said, "Do not hold on to me, because I have not yet ascended to the Father. But go to my brothers and say to them, 'I am ascending to my Father and your Father'" (John 20:17). Prior to this in the Gospel of John, Jesus always referred to God only as "my Father." A fruit of Jesus's resurrection is that we, his followers, now share his intimate relationship with God.

Applying these parables to the process of dying, we might say metaphorically: (1) dying is like the experience of being found by someone who cherishes us; and (2) dying is like finally coming home to a Love that embraces us just as we are. Dying, when imagined as a joyful reunion or homecoming, can quiet any fear we might have of meeting up with a fierce and demanding judge. Christian faith invites us to view life as a journey or pilgrimage; we come from God and are meant to return to God, who is the fulfillment of our deepest longings. In the words of St. Augustine, "You have made us for yourself, O God, and our hearts will be restless until they rest in you

***Parable of the Lost Sheep*** (Luke 15:4–7): To capture the significance of this parable, it helps to imagine being rescued or being reunited with a loved one. Imagine, for example, the joy of a child lost in a crowded department store when she hears the familiar voice of her mother calling her name. Or the great relief and hope of a stranded hiker, struggling with icy weather and dwindling supplies, when he sees the spotlight of a rescue helicopter zero in on him. Might dying be seen metaphorically through the parable of the lost sheep as an experience of being found by someone who loves and cherishes us?

In the parable of the lost sheep, Jesus tells the story of a shepherd who owned a hundred sheep. When he discovers that one is missing, he leaves the ninety-nine in the desert and goes in search of the missing one. As if it were a foregone conclusion and a question not deserving even a moment of thought, Jesus asks his audience, "Which of you, like this shepherd, would fail to leave the rest behind and go after the missing one until it is found?" Arguably, not everyone would share what Jesus implies to be the only reasonable response; after all, does it make good sense to leave the remaining ninety-nine unprotected? It could be argued that the shepherd's decision was a poor one. Would it not be better for the shepherd to cut his losses by building better fences or hiring part-time help to tend his flock? Why jeopardize the remaining sheep by going off in search of the lost one? These considerations do not deter this shepherd, whose single-minded devotion sets him off in search. And then when he finds the missing sheep, he joyfully returns home and sets up a celebration with his friends and neighbors, saying to them, "Rejoice with me, for I have found my sheep that was lost."

The image of the good shepherd was a favorite of the early Christians and remains through the centuries as a consoling reminder of God's love for us. When, on their deathbed, people request that Psalm 23, "The Good Shepherd," be read to them, it may be because it provides such soothing comfort:

> The LORD is my shepherd, I shall not want.
>     He makes me lie down in green pastures;
> he leads me beside still waters;
>     he restores my soul.
> He leads me in right paths
>     for his name's sake.
>
> Even though I walk through the darkest valley,
>     I fear no evil;
> for you are with me;
>     your rod and your staff—
>     they comfort me.

You prepare a table before me
    in the presence of my enemies;
you anoint my head with oil;
    my cup overflows.
Surely goodness and mercy shall follow me
    all the days of my life,
and I shall dwell in the house of the LORD
    my whole life long.

In John's Gospel, Jesus uses this same image of the good shepherd to show his intimate relationship with us. We can imagine the consolation we would feel when at the hour of our death, we hear the words of Jesus reminding us that God, like a good shepherd, cares for us and protects us, the sheep of his flock.

> I am the good shepherd. I know my own and my own know me, just as the Father knows me and I know the Father. And I lay down my life for the sheep.
>
> (John 10:14–15)

> My sheep hear my voice. I know them, and they follow me. I give them eternal life, and they will never perish. No one will snatch them out of my hand.
>
> (John 10:27–28)

Interestingly, at the tomb, Mary Magdalene's recognition of the risen Jesus, whom she mistakenly took for the gardener, was triggered by her hearing him calling her name. Jesus is indeed the good shepherd who knows each by name; they know his voice and they follow him.

**Parable of the Lost Coin** (Luke 15:8–10): This second parable invites us to imagine ourselves as a lost coin that is highly valued. Here Jesus likens God to a woman who misplaced a coin.

As in the parable of the lost sheep, Jesus poses a rhetorical question that seems to have only one reasonable answer. 'What woman having ten silver coins, if she loses one of them, does not light a lamp, sweep the house, and search carefully until she finds it?" This story also ends with a celebration. "When she has found it, she calls together her friends and neighbors, saying, 'Rejoice with me, for I have found the coin that I had lost.' Just so, I tell you, there is joy in the presence of the angels of God over one sinner who repents." Here, Jesus uses a feminine image of God, who is so attached to each of us that she would turn the whole of creation upside down to find us. This account points out that each of us, no matter how ordinary we are, is precious in God's eyes. The woman's delight and joy in finding the lost coin mirror God's delight in us. It is consoling to imagine God's great joy when we, like the lost coin, are found!

***Parable of the Prodigal Son*** (Luke 15:11–32): This parable, perhaps the best known of Jesus's stories, also serves as a metaphor of the dying experience—a way of imagining what the end of life might be like. A father had two sons. The younger of them asked for his share of his inheritance, even though there is no hint that his father was near death. Without hesitation, the father consents to his son's request and supports his desire to leave home in search of fulfillment. This parable likens human life to an unrestricted gift that we receive from the hands of a generous God. Like a loving parent, God gives us life and permits us to freely live our own lives— even though our self-directed journeys, like that of the younger son, may sometimes be misguided. This caring father kept his son in his heart all the while he was away and daily scanned the horizon for the slightest sign of his return. Then one day, he caught sight of his son, and while he was still a long way off, the father was moved with compassion. "He ran and put his arms around him and kissed him." Startled, though relieved by his father's warm welcome, the returning son tried to deliver the apology he had rehearsed: "Father, I have sinned against heaven and before you; I am no longer worthy to be called your son." But his words—full of self-accusing shame—

were muffled by an embrace and drowned out by his father's shouting out orders to the servants, "Quickly, bring out a robe—the best one—and put it on him; put a ring on his finger and sandals on his feet. And get the fatted calf and kill it, and let us eat and celebrate; for this son of mine was dead and is alive again; he was lost and is found." This story could easily be renamed the parable of the extravagantly loving father, for it encapsulates the stunning good news that God loves us like a "prodigal" father, and we, like Jesus, can call God "*Abba*," "papa."

Like the prodigal son who felt ashamed and unworthy, we too can be confident of God's enduring, unshakable love for us, no matter what. This parable provides a glimpse of the immensity of God's love, which embraces the totality of our being, warts and all. Throughout the seasons of our lives—until the hour of our death—the God who causes the sun to shine on the good and the bad, and who lets the rain fall on the just and the unjust, never fails to shower us with abundant grace and acceptance. Perhaps the best-known illustration Jesus gives of the utterly loving nature of God, the parable of the prodigal son invites us to anticipate a happy ending to our own life's story.

# Imaginative Contemplation of Scripture

Luke's Gospel reassures us of God's unconditional love. Like the shepherd, the woman, and the father in these stories, God longingly searches for us; we are objects of God's desire. Simply reading these parables, however, often fails to convey this in a heartfelt and transformative way. To absorb the good news, we need to imaginatively enter into each parable and identify with the missing sheep, the lost coin, and the prodigal son, and then imagine God's joy and delight when we are found and reunited. Actively participating in gospel stories in this way enables us to see with the heart and thus deepen our realization of God's love for us.

A simple three-step process can engage our imagination in praying with Scripture.

> First, read the account of the story, like the story of the prodigal son.
>
> Second, identify with one of the onlookers and describe the event from his or her point of view. Do this as if the event were actually unfolding right now in front of your eyes.
>
> Third, insert yourself into the event by identifying with one of the active participants in the story. With which character in the story of the prodigal son, for instance, do you identify: the younger son, the older son, the father, the servant? As you experience what is happening in the gospel story, be aware of what you are thinking, sensing, and feeling—your entire subjective response.

Capturing the value of contemplating Scripture and imaginatively identifying with gospel characters, the late theologian Bill Spohn wrote, "As we tangibly and visibly move into their narrated encounter with the Lord, we find in ourselves some echo of their response....If the father could welcome home the prodigal son, then my fears of God's anger are without foundation."[1]

# God's Welcome Is Wide

The story of the prodigal son directs our attention to the exuberant and forgiving welcome the son receives. The father's behavior surprises some, who find the father too permissive and soft. Their norms of fairness and justice require that the wayward son be held accountable for squandering his inheritance. Instead, the father embraces his son without hesitation, as if to say, "The only thing that matters is that you have come home." No recriminations, no questions, no guilt trips; only unconditional love and acceptance. This is why the story stands as a dramatic proclamation of the unconditional love that God has for each of us.

An often overlooked dimension of this parable is the deep love the father has for his older son, who is bothered by the gracious welcome given to his brother. He complains that his father has never thrown a party to reward him for his dutiful behavior and devotion. And here this errant and irresponsible son returns, and the fatted calf is slaughtered to honor him. Caught by surprise at his older son's hurt and envy, the father pleads with him to understand. "Son, you are always with me, and all that is mine is yours" (Luke 15:31). We can hear in these words how dismayed and anxious he is to convey the love he has for his dutiful son, who has remained by his side. Whether we identify with the dutiful older son or the wild, adventurous younger son, the parable makes clear that God's love is lavish and wide; it embraces us all, whether we have stayed on the straight and narrow or have strayed from the path.

Both sons faced the challenge of allowing themselves to be loved. The younger son's feelings of shame could have made him push his father away and resist his loving embrace. He could have insisted that he was truly unworthy of love and fit only to return as a hired hand. He could have frustrated his father's desire to love him so lavishly. The older son was challenged to recognize his father's love shown in their intimate sharing of daily life. Blinded by his hurt and envy, he struggled to appreciate the fullness of his father's love, which both he and his brother enjoyed equally, but not in the same way.

That we are so loved by God lies at the core of the Christian message: each of us is the beloved in whom God takes great delight. Too often, we withhold love from ourselves and place a myriad of conditions on our worthiness. An inner voice that says, "I would be lovable *if only* I were more faithful, generous, kind, successful," prevents us from accepting ourselves, as God does, without condition. The gospel, however, tells us that the voice we need to heed is the one that addressed Jesus at his baptism in the Jordan and today seeks to convey the same divine affirmation to each of us: "*You* are my beloved one in whom I take great delight." Thus, theologian Paul Tillich describes faith as "the courage to accept our acceptability despite feelings of unacceptability."[2] Only when we allow this divine affirmation to permeate our hearts and to reverberate throughout our being will we be freed from our fears of meeting God at the hour of our death. The disciple who reclined next to Jesus at the last supper with his head intimately resting on Jesus's chest is referred to as the beloved disciple. Like the disciple John, we too are meant to take on this identity as Jesus's beloved. And because Jesus is the image of the invisible God (Col 1:15), his love reassures us of God's love for each of us.

Yet, we know from our struggles to love ourselves and others that living out of this identity as the beloved is a daily challenge. For most of us, feeling like God's beloved is something we hold tenuously. Moments of doubt make us forget the graciousness of our being, and we need to be reminded of our loveliness. Poet Galway Kinnel eloquently expresses the affirming nature of love in his poem of St. Francis and the sow.

> The bud
> stands for all things
> even for those things that don't flower,
> for everything flowers, from within, of self-blessings
> though sometimes it is necessary
> to reteach a thing its loveliness,
> to put a hand on its brow
> of the flower
> and retell it in words and in touch
> it is lovely

Until it flowers again from within, of self-blessing;
as Saint Francis
put his hand on the creased forehead
of the sow, and told her in word and in touch
blessings of earth on the sow, and the sow
began remembering all down her thick length,
from the earthen snout all the way
through the fodder and slops
to the spiritual curl of the tail,
from hard spininess spiked out from the spine
down through the great broken heart
to the blue milken dreaminess spurting and shuddering
from the fourteen teats into the fourteen mouths
sucking and blowing beneath them:
the long, perfect loveliness of sow.[3]

# Harmful Images of God

For many, their fear of dying stems from a negative image of God and the terror of meeting up with a wrathful God. David Benner, a Christian psychologist and spiritual director, often asks people to try a simple exercise: "Imagine God thinking of you. What do you assume God feels when you come to mind?" A surprising number of people, according to Benner, say "that the first thing they assume God feels is disappointment. Others assume that God feels anger. In both cases, these people are convinced that it is their sin that first catches God's attention." For Benner, these people have it all wrong. "Regardless of what you have come to believe about God based on your life experience," he argues, "the truth is that when God thinks of you, love swells in his heart and a smile comes to his face. God bursts with love for humans."[4]

Benner's words echo those of Julian of Norwich, a fourteenth-century English mystic. "For as truly as we shall be in the bliss of

God without end praising and thanking him, so truly have we been in God's prevision loved and known in his endless purpose from without beginning."[5] When we meet God face-to-face, we will not be plagued with "if only" regrets. Instead, "we shall then clearly see in God the mysteries which are now hidden from us. And then shall none of us be moved to say in any matter: Lord, if it had been so, it would have been well. But we shall all say with one voice: Lord, blessed may you be, because it is so, it is well."[6]

When she wrote those words, Julian was expressing her attitude toward life. Her spirituality is filled with confident hope in a God who loves us and delights in us. In her account of her revelations, she speaks in paradoxical terms of "our precious Mother Jesus," who protects and strengthens us. "Our savior is our true Mother," she writes, "in whom we are endlessly born and out of whom we shall never come."[7] This maternal care never leaves us: "The sweet gracious hands of our Mother are ready and diligent about us," like a caring nurse who attends "to the safety of her child." Julian uses womblike images to express her deep sense of God's compassionate and secure love. We are "enclosed" in the community of the Trinity;[8] God is "our clothing, who wraps and enfolds us for love, embraces us and shelters us, surrounds us for his love."[9] These feminine images serve as lenses through which Julian sees God's profound love for each of us.

# Forgiveness: The End Point of Life

Carl Rogers, the father of client-centered therapy and a major influence in the field of pastoral counseling, had an absolute trust in our individual capacity to choose the good and to develop our human potential. This optimistic view, however, overlooks a key aspect of human nature. We all feel ambivalent at times about growing, changing, and choosing what we know is right. We can remember past sins and times when we hurt others. As we age, these memories can invade our minds, filling us with guilt and making us fear death. Our human weakness, however, need not fill us with fear. As Christians, we believe the good news so graphically illustrated by the three parables in Luke 15, his "lost and found" department—that forgiveness, not perfection, is the end point of human life. Perfection is beyond our reach as fallible human beings. Yes, we are at core good, despite being imperfect.

Consequently, we need not worry; instead, we are called to trust in the forgiving love of God. In the end, we can fully enjoy the unconditional acceptance of God, not because we are flawless, but *in spite of* our imperfections. Our merciful God's gift of forgiveness means that we do not have to measure up to any condition of worth. When forgiveness, and not perfection, is seen as the end point of our lives, we can live with greater acceptance of ourselves. With St. Paul, we are "confident of this, that the one who began a good work" in us "will bring it to completion by the day of Jesus Christ" (Phil 1:6). When our journey reaches its termination, we will be wrapped in God's merciful arms, like the prodigal son.

Because "You are forgiven" will be the final words we will hear, we are freed from the compulsive need to be flawless or faultless and are released from the guilt that accompanies falling short of that goal. "Success and failure are accidental," writes one spiritual writer. "The joy of the Christian is never based on...success but on the knowledge that [our] Redeemer lives."[10] Thus he encourages us to learn to live peacefully to the end of our lives with a certain imperfection:

> The Lord will never ask how successful we were in overcoming particular vice, sin, or imperfection. He will ask us, "Did you humbly and patiently accept this mystery of iniquity in your life? How did you deal with it? Did you learn from it to be patient and humble? Did it teach you to trust not your own ability but My love? Did it

enable you to understand better the mystery of iniquity in the lives of others?[11]

Our lack of perfection will never separate us from God because God's forgiveness is always perfect and total. Thus, the Psalmist sings with confidence, I "trust in the steadfast love of God forever and ever. I will thank you forever, because of what you have done. In the presence of the faithful I will proclaim your name, for it is good" (Ps 52:8–9).

# SPIRITUAL EXERCISES AND REFLECTION

## A. Knowing the Love of God in Our Hearts

In the book *The Shack*, the central character, Mack, questions God: "So why do I have so much fear in my life?"

God: "Because you don't believe. You don't know that we love you. The person who lives by fears will not find freedom in my love. I am not talking about rational fears regarding legitimate dangers, but imagined fears and especially the projection of those into the future. To the degree that those fears have a place in your life, you neither believe I am good nor know deep in your heart that I love you. You sing about it, you talk about it, *but you don't know it.*"[12]

## Some Gospel Paradigms of God's Love

- Parable of the lost sheep (Luke 15:4–7)
- Parable of the lost coin (Luke 15:8–10)
- Parable of the prodigal son (Luke 15:11–32)
- The bent-over woman (Luke 13:10–13)
- The son of the widow of Nain restored to life (Luke 7:11–17)
- The woman and Jesus at Simon's dinner (Luke 7:36–50)
- Zacchaeus, the short tax-collector (Luke 19:1–10)
- The adulterous woman (John 8:1–11)
- Peter, reconciled and re-commissioned (John 21:1–19)
- The good thief (Luke 23:39–43)

# Reflection Guidelines

1. When praying over any of the gospel stories suggested above, either using your imagination or slowly pondering the text, pay attention to how you are moved. What feelings are evoked in you? (*Spiritual Exercises of St. Ignatius*, Annotation no. 6)
2. Which characters do you most identify with and feel attracted to? With which characters do you least identify with and have negative feelings toward?
3. What concerns or issues in your life are reflected in the story?
4. Are you drawn to spend more time with this particular story? In praying with this story, what grace would you like to receive? What desire of your heart do you want God to satisfy? (*Spiritual Exercises of St. Ignatius*, no. 48, What I Want)

# NOTES

## Introduction

1. *Time*, February 22, 2011: 51, 68–71; Jim Oeppen and James W. Vaupel, "Democracy Enhanced: Broken Limits to Life Expectancy," *Science* 296 (May 2002): 1029–31.

2. Dr. Lionel Corbett, Plenary Address at "Jung and Aging: Bringing to Life the Possibilities and Potentials for Vital Aging" Conference, March 28, 2012.

3. Robert C. Atchley, "Spirituality—Age and Life Stage in Spiritual Development," accessed March 22, 2019, http://medicine.jrank.org/pages/1634/Spirituality-Age-life-stage-in-spiritual-development.html.

4. See Jonathan Haidt, *The Happiness Hypothesis*, cited in Nicholas Kristof, "Our Basic Human Pleasures," *New York Times*, Janaury 17, 2010.

5. Dr. Lionel Corbett, "Jung and Aging."

6. See Jonathan Haidt, *The Happiness Hypothesis*.

7. Carl Jung, *Collected Works* (Princeton: Princeton University Press, 2014), vol. 11, par. 114.

8. Joan Chittister, *The Gift of Years: Growing Older Gracefully* (Katonah, NY: BlueBridge, 2008), 47.

9. Lars Tornstam, "Gero-Transcendence: A Theoretical and Empirical Exploration," in *Aging and the Religious Dimension*, ed. L. E. Thomas and S. A. Eisenhandler (Westport, CT: Auburn House, 1994), 203–29.

10. Robert C. Atchley, "Spirituality."

11. Bonnie Ware, "Top 5 Regrets of the Dying," from *AARP*, February 1, 2012.

12. "Seventeenth-Century Nun's Prayer," Bible.org, accessed March 22, 2019, https://bible.org/illustration/seventeenth-century -nuns-prayer.

# Chapter 1

1. Ram Dass, *Still Here: Embracing Aging, Changing, and Dying*, ed. Mark Matousek and Marlene Roeder (New York: River-head Books, 2000), 27.

2. George E. Vaillant, *Aging Well: Surprising Guideposts to a Happy Life from the Landmark Harvard Study of Adult Development* (New York: Little, Brown, and Company, 2002).

3. George E. Vaillant, "Positive Emotions, Spirituality and the Practice of Psychiatry," *Mens Sana Monographs* 6, no. 1 (January–December 2008): 19.

4. Vaillant, "Positive Emotions," 9–10.

5. Rabbi Rami Shapiro, "Roadside Assistance for the Spiritual Traveler," *Spirituality and Health* (July/August 2009): 16.

6. Marcus J. Borg, *The Heart of Christianity: Rediscovering a Life of Faith* (New York: HarperCollins, 2004), 32–33.

7. Today, Christian spirituality clearly acknowledges the important contribution of the imagination to prayer and spiritual growth. The use of images is valued as a needed complement to an early contemplative tradition that stresses the inadequacy of the senses and imagination to grasp the Mystery of God. Thus the journey of faith can follow along two distinct paths: the way of images and the imageless way. While Christians often value one approach over the other, holding both approaches to God in a creative tension is important. Each can contribute to our relationship with God. Both approaches enrich our Christian faith and must be retained for the sake of balance and integrity. The imageless way reminds us that God is always more than the human mind can ever conceive or imagine. Any real knowledge of God must be received as a gift of divine disclosure. As limited creatures, we can only bow in awe and adoration before the infinite Mystery of God and wait to be visited.

However, the way of images reminds us how blessed we are that God has chosen to reveal God's self to us. The use of images and words, especially those found in Scripture, can transport us into the mysteries of faith. This approach affirms that divine self-disclosure has occurred in history and reached its high point in the person of Jesus Christ and his message.

Together both paths offer Christian faith a way of knowing something of the nature of God, while simultaneously respecting the illimitable Mystery of God. We need to move back and forth between using images to support our faith, on the one hand, and acknowledging that our impoverished words and images can never be equated with the reality of God, on the other. Because our words, no matter how eloquent or poetic, ultimately fail us, we must regularly put aside our theological lexicon and approach the living God with open minds and dependent hearts.

8. Gregory Baum, *Man Becoming: God in Secular Experience* (New York: Herder and Herder, 1971), 194–95.

9. Peter Enns, *The Sin of Certainty: Why God Desires Our Trust More Than Our "Correct" Beliefs* (New York: HarperCollins, 2016), 21 (emphasis in the original).

10. Borg, *The Heart of Christianity*, 31–34.

11. Enns, *The Sin of Certainty*, 22.

12. Denise Levertov, *Selected Poems*, ed. Paul A. Lacy (New York: New Directions, 2002), 142.

13. As quoted in Michael Ford, *Wounded Prophet: A Portrait of Henri J. Nouwen* (New York: Doubleday, 1999), 22.

14. Denise Levertov, *Selected Poems*, ed. Paul A. Lacy (New York: New Directions, 2002), 176.

15. Enns, *The Sin of Certainty*, 205.

16. Cory Taylor, *Dying: A Memoir* (Portland: Tin House Books, 2016), 37.

17. Taylor, *Dying: A Memoir*, 36.

18. Borg, *The Heart of Christianity*, 35.

19. As quoted in Kathleen Norris, *The Cloister Walk* (New York: Riverhead Books, 1996), 222.

20. Pierre Teilhard de Chardin quoted in *Hearts on Fire: Praying with Jesuits*, ed. Michael Harter (St. Louis: The Institute of Jesuit Sources, 1993), 97.

21. Michael J. Buckley, *What Do You Seek? The Questions of Jesus as Challenge and Promise* (Grand Rapids, MI: Eerdmans, 2016), 129.

22. Quoted in Martha E. Stortz, "The School of Hope," *Santa Clara* (Winter 2006).

23. Antony F. Campbell, *God First Loved Us: The Challenge of Accepting Unconditional Love* (Mahwah, NJ: Paulist Press, 2000), 88.

# Chapter 2

1. James Whitehead, "Priesthood: A Crisis of Belonging," in *Being a Priest Today*, ed. Donald J. Goergen (Collegeville, MN: Liturgical Press, 1992), 18.

2. Whitehead, "Priesthood," 18.

3. Eugene H. Peterson, *The Jesus Way: A Conversation on the Ways that Jesus is the Way* (Grand Rapids, MI: Eerdmans, 2007), 55.

4. Peterson, *The Jesus Way*, 44.

5. Gerard Manley Hopkins, "As Kingfishers Catch Fire," in *Poems of Gerard Manley Hopkins*, ed. Robert Bridges (London: Humphrey Milford, 1918).

6. Karl Rahner, *The Practice of Faith: A Handbook of Contemporary Spirituality*, ed. Karl Lehmann and Albert Raffelt, trans. John Griffiths (New York: Crossroad, 1983), 22.

7. Rahner, *The Practice of Faith*, 8. See also Janet K. Ruffing, *Spiritual Direction: Beyond the Beginnings* (Mahwah, NJ: Paulist Press, 2000), 67–70.

8. Michael J. Buckley, *What Do You Seek? The Questions of Jesus as Challenge and Promise* (Grand Rapids, MI: Eerdmans, 2016), 88.

9. Becky Garrison, "Where Is God?," in *Luminos: Faith & Light for the Journey* 122, no.1 (Spring 2009): 16.

10. Garrison, "Where Is God?," 16.

11. Rabbi Lawrence Kushner, *Introduction to Jewish Spirituality*, a three-part video series produced for use with the Professional Development Training Program (PDTC) sponsored by the United States Navy Chaplain's Corps for Sea Service Chaplains in 1997.

12. Belden C. Lane, "Rabbinical Stories: A Primer on Theological Method," *Christian Century* 98:41 (December 16, 1981): 1307.

13. Written by a student in an Ignatian Spirituality course at Loyola Marymount University and used with her permission.

# Chapter 3

1. Atul Gawande, *Being Mortal: Medicine and What Matters in the End* (New York: Henry Holt, 2014), 35.

2. Ram Dass, *Still Here: Embracing Aging, Changing, and Dying*, ed. Mark Matousek and Marlene Roeder (New York: Riverhead Books, 2000), 65.

3. Juliet Macur, "Scott Hamilton Was Demoted as an Olympic Broadcaster. Don't Feel Sorry for Him," *New York Times*, February 18, 2018.

4. Cricket Cooper, *Chemo Pilgrim: An 18-Week Journey of Healing and Holiness* (New York: Church Publishing, 2017), 2.

5. Cooper, *Chemo Pilgrim*, 61.

6. Copyright © 2005 Contemplative Outreach, LTD.

7. Richard Rohr, "Richard Rohr's Daily Meditation," Friday, September 1, 2017.

8. Belden C. Lane, "Rabbinical Stories: A Primer on Theological Method," *Christian Century* 98, no. 41 (December 16, 1984): 1308–9.

9. Dass, *Still Here*, 50.

10. Cooper, *Chemo Pilgrim*, 114–15.

11. John Leland, *Happiness Is a Choice You Make: Lessons from a Year among the Oldest Old* (New York: Farrar, Straus and Giroux, 2018), 60.

12. Colleen Morton Busch, *Fire Monks: Zen Mind Meets Wildfire* (New York: Penguin Books, 2012), 243–44.

13. Taken from Anthony de Mello, *Wellsprings: A Book of Spiritual Exercises* (Garden City, NY: Doubleday, 1986), 192–93.

# Chapter 4

1. Atul Gawande, *Being Mortal: Medicine and What Matters in the End* (New York: Henry Holt, 2014), 55.

2. Judith Viorst, *Necessary Losses: The Loves, Illusions, Dependencies, and Impossible Expectations That All of Us Have to Give Up in Order to Grow* (New York: Ballantine Books, 1986), 3.

3. Viorst, *Necessary Losses*, 2.

4. John Leland, *Happiness Is a Choice You Make: Lessons from a Year among the Oldest Old* (New York: Farrar, Straus and Giroux, 2018), 134.

5. Leland, *Happiness Is a Choice You Make*, 134.

6. Phillip Bennett, *Let Yourself Be Loved* (Mahwah, NJ: Paulist Press, 1997), 36.

7. Cf. Gerald A. Arbuckle, "Letting Go in Hope: A Spirituality for a Chaotic World," in *Handbook of Spirituality for Ministers: Perspectives for the 21st Century*, vol. 2, ed. Robert J. Wicks (Mahwah: Paulist Press, 2000), 120–33.

8. Wendy M. Wright, "The Long, Lithe Limbs of Hope," in *Weavings* 14, no. 6 (November/December 1999): 13.

9. Peter Enns, *The Sin of Certainty: Why God Desires Our Trust More than Our "Correct" Beliefs* (New York: HarperCollins, 2016), 163.

10. Arbuckle, "Letting Go in Hope," 121.

11. Ram Dass, *Still Here: Embracing Aging, Changing, and Dying*, ed. Mark Matousek and Marlene Roeder (New York: Riverhead Books, 2000), 126.

12. Bob Pool, "Passenger's Fancy," *Los Angeles Times*, July 23, 1996, B1.

# Chapter 5

1. Rabbi Joshua L. Liebman, as cited in John Leland, *Happiness Is a Choice You Make: Lessons from a Year among the Oldest Old* (New York: Farrar, Straus and Giroux, 2018), 46.

2. Sherwin B. Nuland, *How We Die: Reflections on Life's Final Chapter* (New York: Knopf, 1993), 10.

3. Nuland, *How We Die*, 10.

4. Susan S. Jorgensen, *The Second Bookend: Completing a Life* (San Bernardino: Applecart Press, 2016), 25.

5. Rachel Harris, PhD, in Jorgensen, *The Second Bookend*, 7.

6. Stephen Levine, *A Year to Live: How to Live This Year as If It Were Your Last* (New York: Three Rivers Press, 1997), 4.

7. Stephen Battaglio, "It Was a Wonderful Life," *Los Angeles Times*, June 9, 2018, C2.

8. Mary Oliver, from *New and Selected Poems*, vol. 1 (Boston: Beacon Press, 1992).

9. T. S. Eliot, "Ash Wednesday," in *The Complete Poems and Plays, 1909–1950* (San Diego: Harcourt, Brace & Co., 1971), 67.

10. As quoted in Ram Dass, *Still Here: Embracing Aging, Changing, and Dying*, ed. Mark Matousek and Marlene Roeder (New York: Riverhead Books, 2000), 75.

11. As quoted in Dass, *Still Here*, 75.

12. Quoted in Martha E. Stortz, "The School of Hope," *Santa Clara*, Winter 2006.

13. Stortz, "The School of Hope."

14. Stortz, "The School of Hope."

15. Gerard Manley Hopkins, "The Leaden Echo and the Golden Echo," in *Poems and Prose of Gerard Manley Hopkins*, ed. W. N. Gardner (Baltimore: Penguin, 1953), 53–54.

16. Nuland, *How We Die*, 3.

17. Atul Gawande, *Being Mortal: Medicine and What Matters in the End* (New York: Henry Holt, 2014), 249.

18. Ira Byock, *Dying Well: Peace and Possibilities at the End of Life* (New York: Riverhead Books, 1997), xiv.

19. Levine, *A Year to Live*, 26.

20. William Shakespeare, *Hamlet*, Act 5, Scene 2.

21. Dermot Lane, "Death, the Self, Memory, and Hope," in *Handbook of Spirituality for Ministers: Perspectives for the 21st Century*, vol. 2, ed. Robert J. Wicks (Mahwah, NJ: Paulist Press, 2000), 100.

22. Marcus J. Borg, *Jesus: Uncovering the Life, Teachings, and Relevance of a Religious Revolutionary* (New York: HarperCollins, 2008), 58 (emphasis in the original).

23. Julian of Norwich, *The Revelations of Divine Love or Showings*, chap. 5, as quoted in Jeffrey D. Imbach, *The Recovery of Love: Mysticism and the Addictive Society* (New York: Crossroad, 1992), 51.

24. Julian of Norwich, *The Revelations of Divine Love or Showings*, chap. 5.

25. Adapted from a reflection proposed by Anthony de Mello, *Hearts on Fire: Praying with Jesuits* (St. Louis: Institute of Jesuit Sources, 1993), 18–19.

# Chapter 6

1. Ram Dass, *Still Here: Embracing Aging, Changing, and Dying*, ed. Mark Matousek and Marlene Roeder (New York: Riverhead Books, 2000), 51.

2. John Edgar Widerman, *Brothers and Keepers* (1984), as cited by Robert C. Roberts, "The Blessings of Gratitude: A Conceptual Analysis," in *The Psychology of Gratitude*, ed. Robert A. Emmons and Michael E. McCullough (New York: Oxford University Press, 2004), 70.

3. Irvin D. Yalom, *Staring at the Sun: Overcoming the Terror of Death* (San Francisco: Jossey-Bass, 2008), 145–46.

4. John Leland, *Happiness Is a Choice You Make: Lessons from a Year among the Oldest Old* (New York: Farrar, Straus and Giroux, 2018), 15–17.

5. Jim Harbaugh, *A 12-Step Approach to the Spiritual Exercises of St. Ignatius* (Kansas City: Sheed & Ward, 1997), 28.

6. Ram Dass, *Still Here*, 41.

7. Lewis B. Smedes, *Forgive and Forget: Healing the Hurts We Don't Deserve* (San Francisco: HarperSanFrancisco, 1984), 22–23.

8. Ram Dass, *Still Here*, 122.

9. Terri Mifek, "Away from the Comfort Zone," in *Living Faith: Daily Catholic Devotions* (Fenton, MO: Creative Communications for the Parish, 2009), vol. 25, no. 1, June 22, 2009.

10. Gregory Boyle, *Barking to the Choir: The Power of Radical Kinship* (New York: Simon and Schuster, 2017), 37–38.

11. Helen Mallicoat, "I Am," in *Listen for the Lord* (Kansas City, MO: Hallmark Cards, Inc., 1977).

12. Johann Christoph Arnold, *Seventy Times Seven: The Power of Forgiveness* (Farmington, PA: The Plough Publishing House of the Bruderhof Foundation, 1997), 24.

# Chapter 7

1. Patrick J. Skerrett, "Is Retirement Good for Health or Bad for It?," Harvard Health Blog, December 10, 2012, last

updated October 29, 2015, https://www.health.harvard.edu/blog/is-retirement-good-for-health-or-bad-for-it-201212105625.

2. Louis Cozolino, *Timeless: Nature's Formula for Health and Longevity* (New York: W. W. Norton, 2018), 29.

3. Ram Dass, *Still Here: Embracing Aging, Changing, and Dying*, ed. Mark Matousek and Marlene Roeder (New York: Riverhead Books, 2000), 102.

4. George Herbert, "Affliction (I)," in *George Herbert: The Country Parson, The Temple*, ed. John Wall, Classics of Western Spirituality (Mahwah, NJ: Paulist Press, 1981), 161. As quoted in "George Herbert at Bemerton," by Deborah Smith Douglas in *Weavings* 14, no. 3 (May/June 1999): 21.

5. George Herbert, "The Flower," in *George Herbert: The Country Parson, The Temple*, 23.

6. Cozolino, *Timeless*, 62.

7. As quoted in Louis Cozolino, *Timeless*, 59.

8. L. Burton and C. Devries, "Challenges and Rewards: African American Grandparents as Surrogate Parents," in *Generations* 16:51–54, as quoted in Louis Cozolino, *Timeless*, 64.

9. Cozolino, *Timeless*, 66–67

10. Cozolino, *Timeless*, 37.

11. Cozolino, *Timeless*, 38.

12. Melissa Healy, "Britain Makes Loneliness a Cabinet-Level Concern," *The Los Angeles Times*, January 26, 2018, A4.

13. Healy, "Britain Makes Loneliness a Cabinet-Level Concern."

14. Healy, "Britain Makes Loneliness a Cabinet-Level Concern."

15. Ram Dass, *Still Here*, 107.

16. Jean Vanier in *The Heart Has Its Reasons* (alternative title: *Jean Vanier and l'Arche*), a video-recording by Martin Doblmeier (Mt. Vernon, VA: Journey Communications, 1984).

17. Robert Wicks, *After Fifty: Spiritually Embracing Your Own Wisdom Years* (Mahwah, NJ: Paulist Press, 1997), 38.

18. Henri Nouwen, *Out of Solitude* (Notre Dame: Ave Maria Press, 1974), 36.

19. Lawrence Kushner, *Honey from the Rock: Visions of Jewish Mystical Renewal* (Woodstock, VT: Jewish Lights Publishing, 1994), 72–75.

20. Kushner, *Honey from the Rock*, 74.

21. Kushner, *Honey from the Rock*, 73.

22. "Prayer of St. Francis," in *Today's Missal: Music Issue* (Portland: Oregon Catholic Press, 1999), no. 695.

23. Attributed to Pedro Arrupe, SJ, from *Finding God in All Things: A Marquette Prayer Book*, © 2009 Marquette University.

# Chapter 8

1. John Leland, *Happiness Is a Choice You Make: Lessons from a Year among the Oldest Old* (New York: Farrar, Straus and Giroux, 2018), 35.

2. Anthony de Mello, *One-Minute Wisdom* (Garden City, NY: Doubleday, 1985), 24–25.

3. Leland, *Happiness Is a Choice You Make*, 22.

4. Neal Krause, "Gratitude toward God, Stress, and Health in Late Life," *Research on Aging* 28, no. 2 (March 2006): 163–83.

5. Leland, *Happiness Is a Choice You Make*, 14.

6. Leland, *Happiness Is a Choice You Make*, 13.

7. Dorothy Foltz-Gray, "What Really Makes Us Happy," *Prevention* 58, no. 2 (February 2006): 156–63.

8. Patricia Schneider, "The Patience of Ordinary Things," from *Another River: New and Selected Poems*, Amherst Writers and Artists Press, 2005.

9. Nikos Kazantzakis, *Zorba the Greek*, trans. Carl Wildman (New York: Simon and Schuster, 1952), 51.

10. Denise Levertov, *Selected Poems*, ed. Paul A. Lacy (New York: New Directions, 2002), 192.

11. See www.goodreads.com/quotes/show/12207 (accessed April 5, 2019).

12. Irvin Yalom, *Staring at the Sun: Overcoming the Terror of Death* (San Francisco: Jossey-Bass, 2008), 135–36.

13. Leland, *Happiness Is a Choice You Make*, 37.

14. Leland, *Happiness Is a Choice You Make*, 18.

15. Philip C. Watkins, "Gratitude and Subjective Well-Being," in *The Psychology of Gratitude*, ed. Robert A. Emmons and Michael E. McCullough (New York: Oxford University Press, 2004), 180.

16. Watkins, "Gratitude and Subjective Well-Being," 180.

17. Elizabeth Gray Vining quoted in Catherine Whitmire, *Plain Living: A Quaker Path to Simplicity* (Notre Dame: Sorin Books, 2001), 68.

18. Monica Furlong, "A Spirituality of Aging?," in *Reflections on Aging and Spiritual Growth*, ed. Andrew J. Weaver, Harold G. Koenig, and Phyllis C. Roe (Nashville: Abingdon Press, 1998), 46.

19. M. Basil Pennington, "Long on the Journey," in Weaver, Koenig, and Roe, *Reflections on Aging and Spiritual Growth*, 30.

20. Marilyn Chandler McEntyre, "Growing in Grace," *Weavings: A Journal of Christian Spiritual Life* 23, no. 1 (January/February 2008): 8.

21. McEntyre, "Growing in Grace," 8.

22. Roberta C. Bondi, *In Ordinary Times: Healing the Wounds of the Heart* (Nashville: Abingdon Press, 1996), 22.

23. Bondi, *In Ordinary Times*, 22.

24. Bondi, *In Ordinary Times*, 23.

25. Bondi, *In Ordinary Times*, 24.

26. Adapted from Stephen Levin, *A Year to Live: How to Live This Year as If It Were Your Last* (New York: Bell Tower), 82–83.

# Chapter 9

1. William C. Spohn, "The Biblical Theology of the Pastoral Letter and Ignatian Contemplation," *Studies in the Spirituality of Jesuits*, 17, no. 4 (1985): 8–9.

2. Paul Tillich, *The Courage to Be* (New Haven: Yale University Press, 1952), 164–65, 172–73.

3. Galway Kinnel, "St. Francis and the Sow," in *Mortal Acts, Mortal Words* (Boston: Houghton Mifflin Company, 1980), 9.

4. David G. Benner, *Surrender to Love: Discovering the Heart of Christian Spirituality* (Downers Grove, IL: Intervarsity Press, 2003), 15–16.

5. Julian of Norwich, *Showings*, chap. 85.

6. Julian of Norwich, *Showings*, chap. 85.

7. Julian of Norwich, *Showings*, chap. 57.

8. Julian of Norwich, *Showings*, chap. 61.

9. Julian of Norwich, *Showings*, chap. 5.

10. Adrian van Kaam, *Religion and Personality* (Denville, NJ: Dimension Books, 1980), 15.

11. van Kaam, *Religion and Personality*, 15.

12. William Paul Young, *The Shack: Where Tragedy Confronts Eternity* (Newbury Park, CA: Windblown Media, 2007), 144.